300 Year Calendar

1760 to 2060

Jack S. Koay, M.D.
Mary Ellen Tekieli Koay, Ph.D.

authorHOUSE™

1663 LIBERTY DRIVE, SUITE 200
BLOOMINGTON, INDIANA 47403
(800) 839-8640
WWW.AUTHORHOUSE.COM

First published by AuthorHouse 12/06/05

ISBN: 1-4208-8637-1 (sc)

Library of Congress Control Number: 2005908428

Printed in the United States of America
Bloomington, Indiana

This book is printed on acid-free paper.

Author's Note

Since the publication of this convenient "300 Year Calendar" book in July 1986 we have had hundreds of requests for additional copies.   Unfortunately, this original book has been out of print for a long time.

With the encouragement of our friends we have decided to make the second edition of this "fun book" to meet their requests.

In this edition we added the Koay Calendar Formula.

With this Formula and with the "Constant Numbers" of 300 years provided, we believe any one could find out the day of the week from the years of 1760 to 2060 in a split second.

In addition Federal Legal Public Holidays are revised and extended from the year 2005 to the year 2025.

Hopefully, this edition will bring more enjoyment and "cognitive reserve" to your healthy brain through mental exercise from the Koay Formula and the Constant Numbers.

The more you practice the Koay Formula the faster you will get your answers. Practice makes perfect.

Enjoy your leisure time with us again!!

July 2005

Table of Contents

Federal Legal Public Holidays

	2005	2006	2007	2008	2009	2010	2011	2012	2013	2014	2015
New Year's Day	Sat Jan. 1	Sun Jan. 1	Mon Jan. 1	Tue Jan. 1	Thu Jan. 1	Fri Jan. 1	Sat Jan. 1	Sun Jan. 1	Tue Jan. 1	Wed Jan. 1	Thu Jan. 1
Martin L. King Day	Mon Jan. 17	Mon Jan. 16	Mon Jan. 15	Mon Jan. 21	Mon Jan. 19	Mon Jan. 18	Mon Jan. 17	Mon Jan. 16	Mon Jan. 21	Mon Jan. 20	Mon Jan. 19
President's Day	Mon Feb. 21	Mon Feb. 20	Mon Feb. 19	Mon Feb. 18	Mon Feb. 16	Mon Feb. 15	Mon Feb. 21	Mon Feb. 20	Mon Feb. 18	Mon Feb. 17	Mon Feb. 16
Memorial Day	Mon May-30	Mon May-29	Mon May-28	Mon May-26	Mon May-25	Mon May-31	Mon May-30	Mon May-28	Mon May-27	Mon May-26	Mon May-25
Independence Day	Mon July-04	Tue July-04	Wed July-04	Fri July-04	Sat July-04	Sun July-04	Mon July-04	Wed July-04	Thu July-04	Fri July-04	Sat July-04
Labor Day	Mon Sept. 5	Mon Sept. 4	Mon Sept. 3	Mon Sept. 1	Mon Sept. 7	Mon Sept. 6	Mon Sept. 5	Mon Sept. 3	Mon Sept. 2	Mon Sept. 1	Mon Sept. 7
Columbus Day	Mon Oct. 10	Mon Oct. 9	Mon Oct. 8	Mon Oct. 13	Mon Oct. 12	Mon Oct. 11	Mon Oct. 10	Mon Oct. 8	Mon Oct. 11	Mon Oct. 13	Mon Oct. 12
Veterans' Day	Fri Nov. 11	Sat Nov. 11	Sun Nov. 11	Tue Nov. 11	Wed Nov. 11	Thu Nov. 11	Fri Nov. 11	Sat Nov. 11	Mon Nov. 11	Tue Nov. 11	Wed Nov. 11
Thanksgiving Day	Thu Nov. 24	Thu Nov. 23	Thu Nov. 22	Thu Nov. 27	Thu Nov. 26	Thu Nov. 25	Thu Nov. 24	Thu Nov. 22	Thu Nov. 28	Thu Nov. 27	Thu Nov. 26
Christmas	Sun Dec. 25	Mon Dec. 25	Tue Dec. 25	Thu Dec. 25	Fri Dec. 25	Sat Dec. 25	Sun Dec. 25	Tue Dec. 25	Wed Dec. 25	Thu Dec. 25	Fri Dec. 25

Federal Legal Public Holidays

	2016	2017	2018	2019	2020	2021	2022	2023	2024	2025
New Year's Day	Fri Jan. 1	Sun Jan. 1	Mon Jan. 1	Tue Jan. 1	Wed Jan. 1	Fri Jan. 1	Sat Jan. 1	Sun Jan. 1	Mon Jan. 1	Wed Jan. 1
Martin L. King Day	Mon Jan. 18	Mon Jan. 16	Mon Jan. 15	Mon Jan. 21	Mon Jan. 20	Mon Jan. 18	Mon Jan. 17	Mon Jan. 16	Mon Jan. 15	Mon Jan. 20
President's Day	Mon Feb. 15	Mon Feb. 20	Mon Feb. 19	Mon Feb. 18	Mon Feb. 17	Mon Feb. 15	Mon Feb. 21	Mon Feb. 20	Mon Feb. 19	Mon Feb. 17
Memorial Day	Mon May-30	Mon May-29	Mon May-28	Mon May-27	Mon May-25	Mon May-31	Mon May-30	Mon May-29	Mon May-27	Mon May-26
Independence Day	Mon July-04	Tue July-04	Wed July-04	Thu July-04	Sat July-04	Sun July-04	Mon July-04	Tue July-04	Thu July-04	Fri July-04
Labor Day	Mon Sept. 5	Mon Sept. 4	Mon Sept. 3	Mon Sept. 2	Mon Sept. 7	Mon Sept. 6	Mon Sept. 5	Mon Sept. 4	Mon Sept. 2	Mon Sept. 1
Columbus Day	Mon Oct. 10	Mon Oct. 9	Mon Oct. 8	Mon Oct. 14	Mon Oct. 12	Mon Oct. 11	Mon Oct. 10	Mon Oct. 9	Mon Oct. 14	Mon Oct. 13
Veterans' Day	Fri Nov. 11	Sat Nov. 11	Sun Nov. 11	Mon Nov. 11	Wed Nov. 11	Thu Nov. 11	Fri Nov. 11	Sat Nov. 11	Mon Nov. 11	Tue Nov. 11
Thanksgiving Day	Thu Nov. 24	Thu Nov. 23	Thu Nov. 22	Thu Nov. 28	Thu Nov. 26	Thu Nov. 25	Thu Nov. 24	Thu Nov. 23	Thu Nov. 28	Thu Nov. 27
Christmas	Sun Dec. 25	Mon Dec. 25	Tue Dec. 25	Wed Dec. 25	Fri Dec. 25	Sat Dec. 25	Sun Dec. 25	Mon Dec. 25	Wed Dec. 25	Thu Dec. 25

Year: **1760**

	JAN							MAY							SEPT					
Sun	Mon	Tue	Wed	Thu	Fri	Sat	Sun	Mon	Tue	Wed	Thu	Fri	Sat	Sun	Mon	Tue	Wed	Thu	Fri	Sat

(calendar grid, January–December 1760, arranged in three rows of four months each: JAN/MAY/SEPT, FEB/JUNE/OCT, MAR/JULY/NOV, APR/AUG/DEC)

Year: **1761**

(calendar grid, January–December 1761)

Year: **1762**

(calendar grid, January–December 1762)

Year: **1763**

(calendar grid, January–December 1763)

Year: **1764**

(calendar grid, January–December 1764)

Year: **1765**

(calendar grid, January–December 1765)

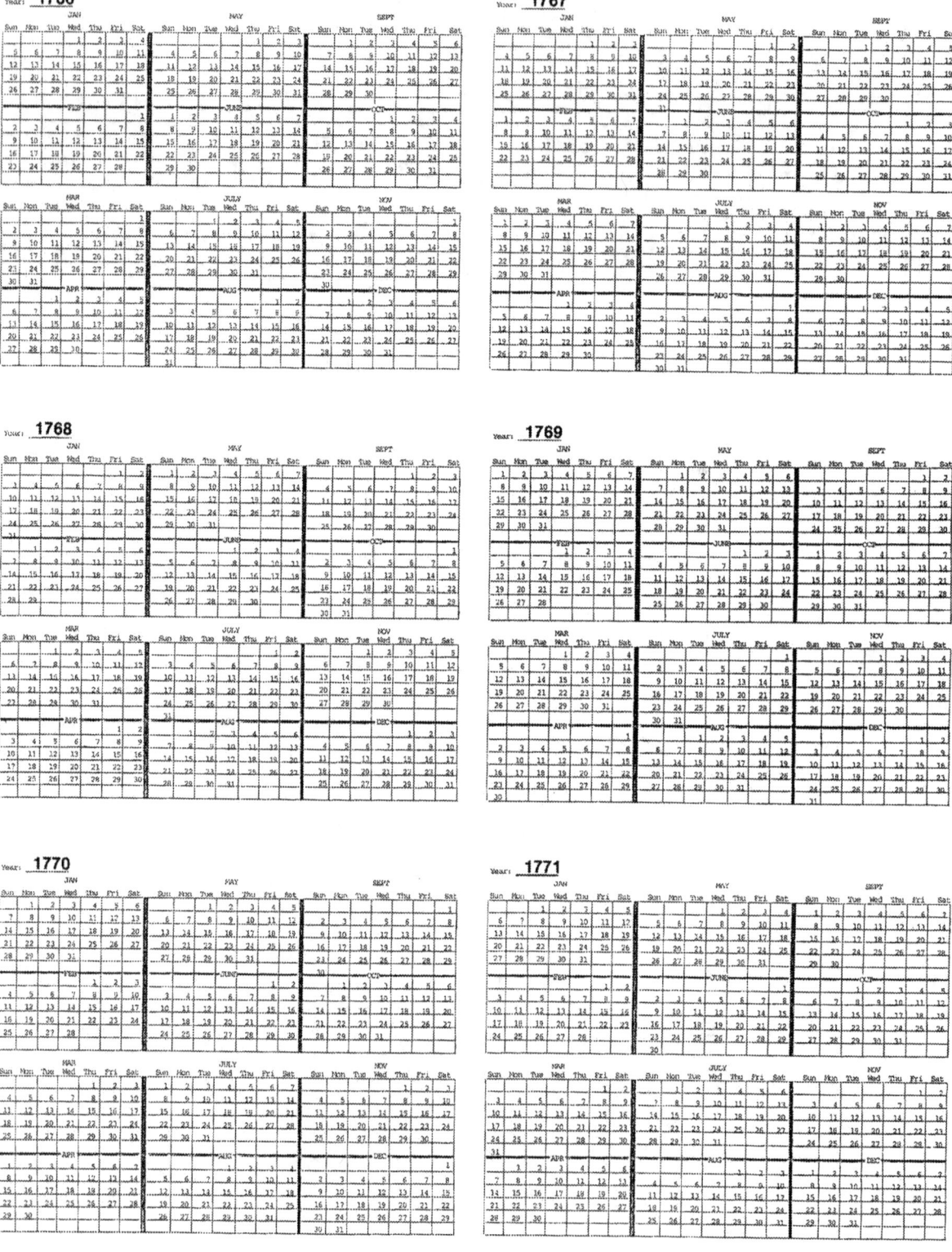

4

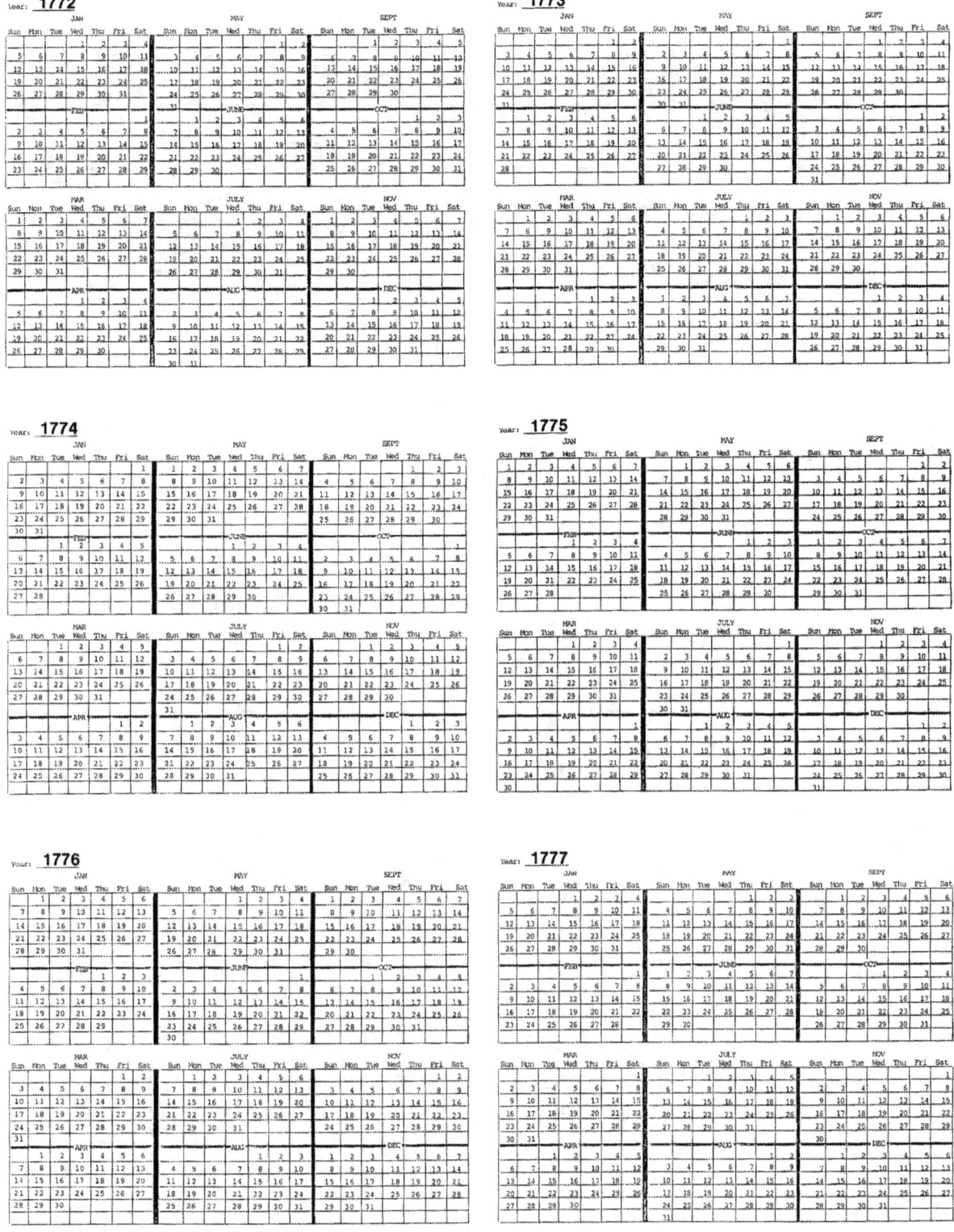

Year: **1772**

Year: **1773**

Year: **1774**

Year: **1775**

Year: **1776**

Year: **1777**

Year: **1778**

JAN MAY SEPT
FEB JUNE OCT
MAR JULY NOV
APR AUG DEC

Year: **1779**

JAN MAY SEPT
FEB JUNE OCT
MAR JULY NOV
APR AUG DEC

Year: **1780**

JAN MAY SEPT
FEB JUNE OCT
MAR JULY NOV
APR AUG DEC

Year: **1781**

JAN MAY SEPT
FEB JUNE OCT
MAR JULY NOV
APR AUG DEC

Year: **1782**

JAN MAY SEPT
FEB JUNE OCT
MAR JULY NOV
APR AUG DEC

Year: **1783**

JAN MAY SEPT
FEB JUNE OCT
MAR JULY NOV
APR AUG DEC

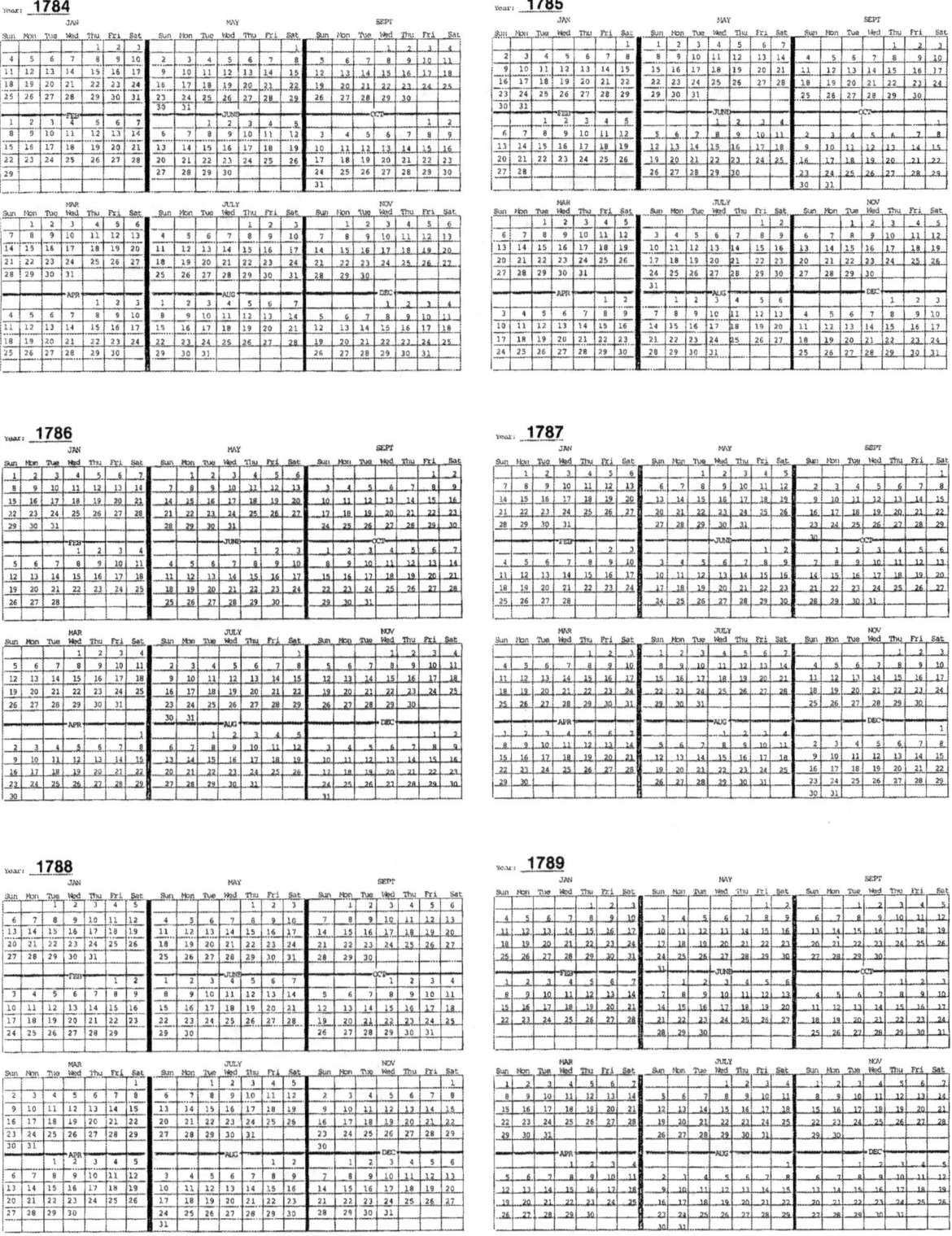

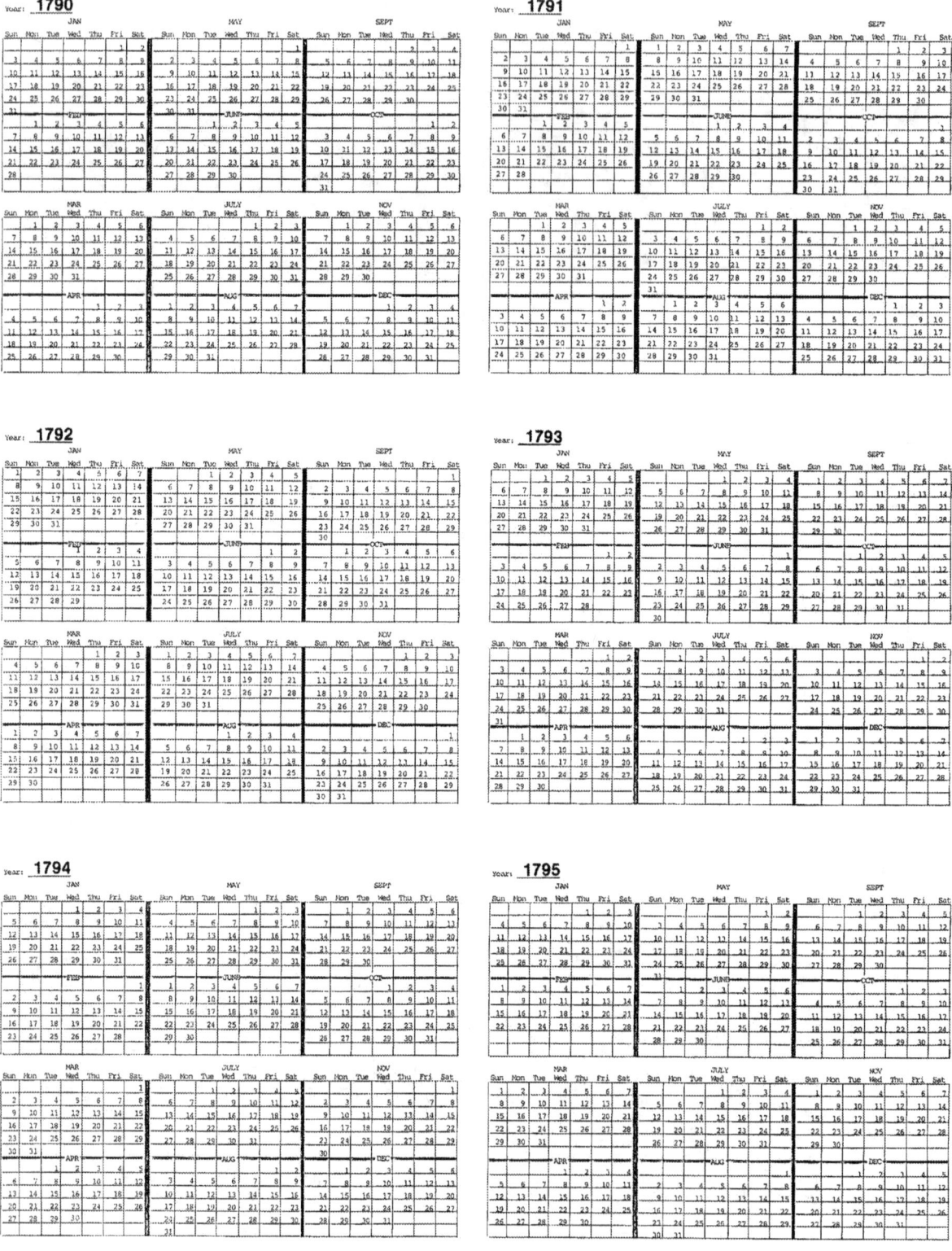

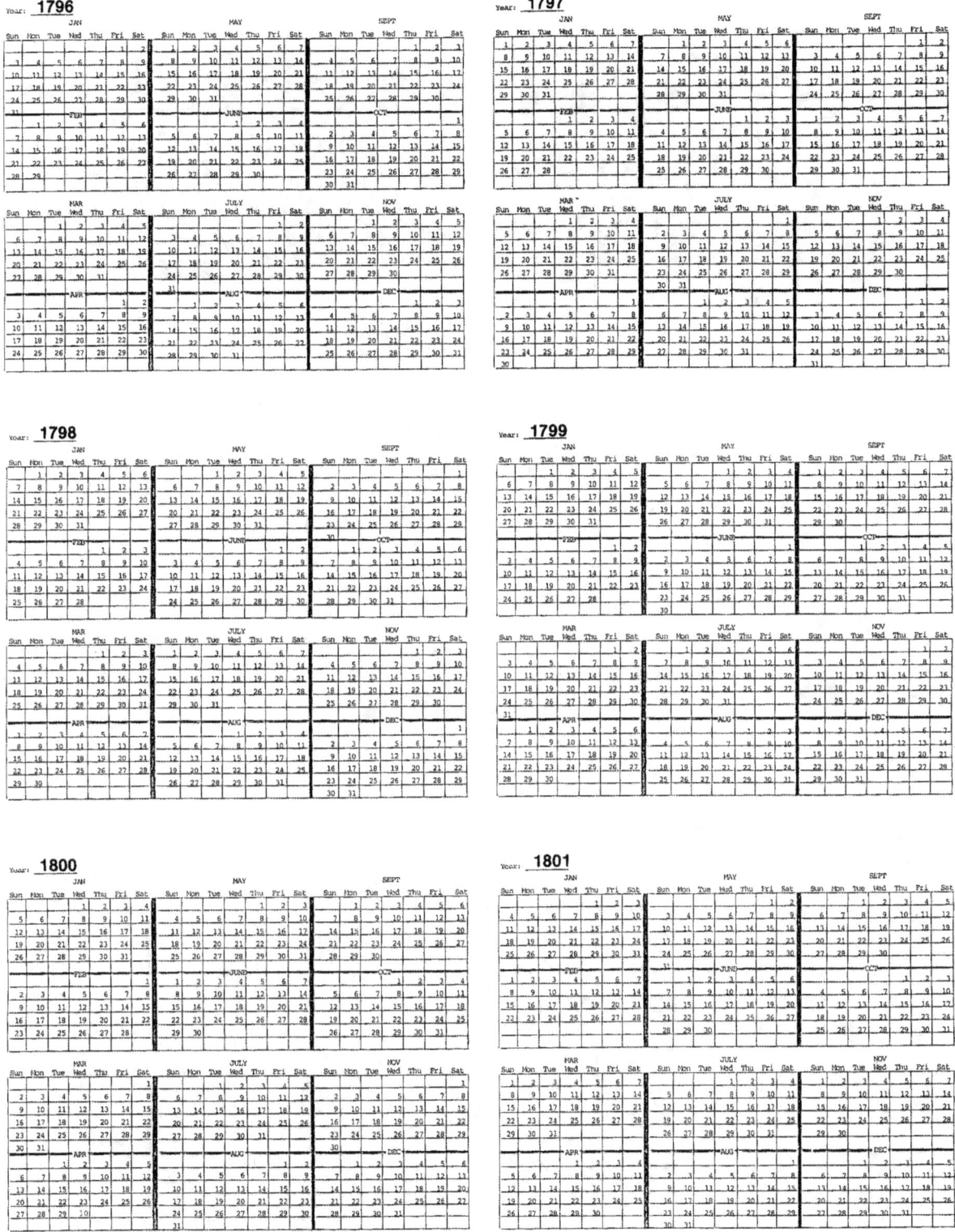

Year: **1802**

Year: **1803**

Year: **1804**

Year: **1805**

Year: **1806**

Year: **1807**

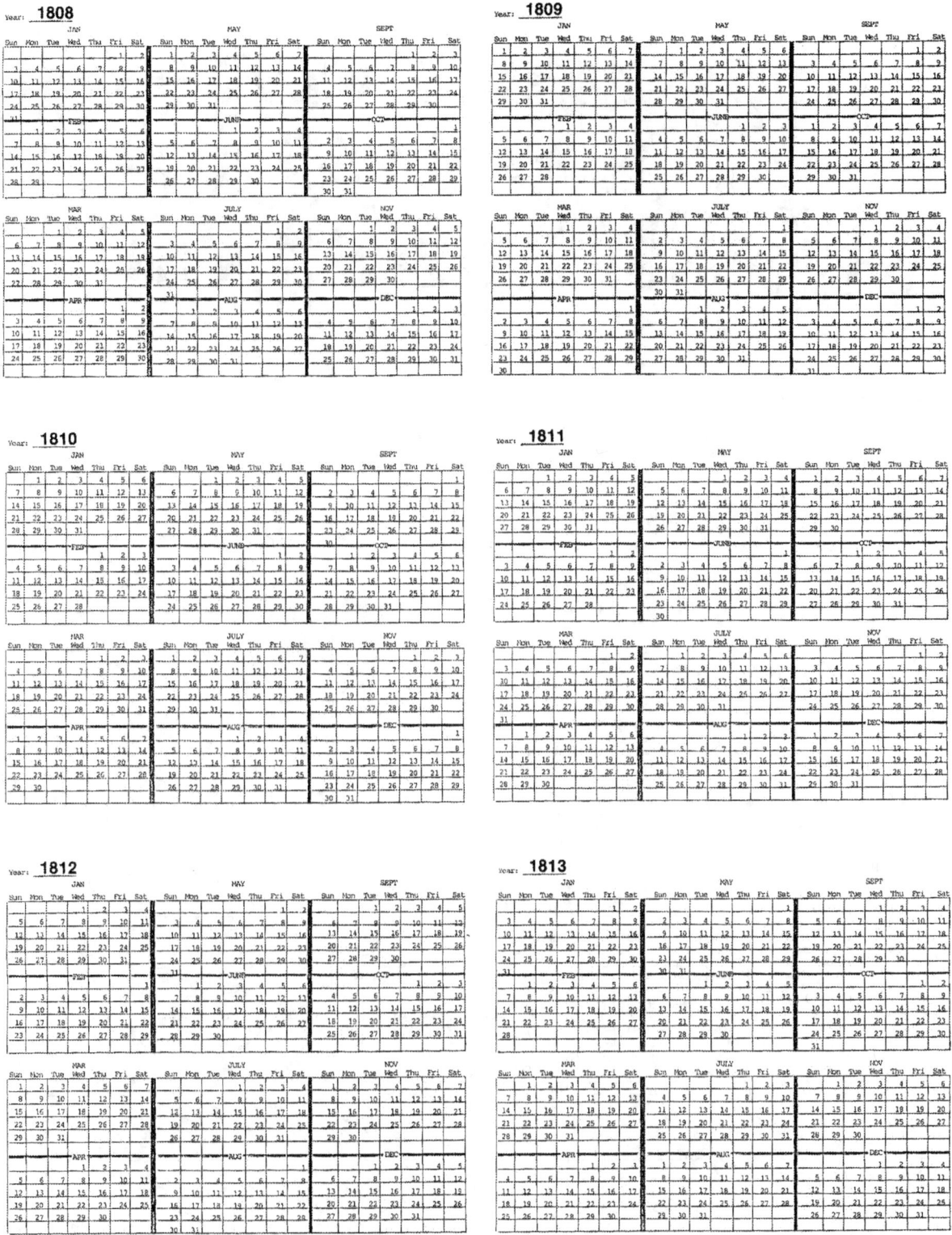

Year: **1814**

Year: **1815**

Year: **1816**

Year: **1817**

Year: **1818**

Year: **1819**

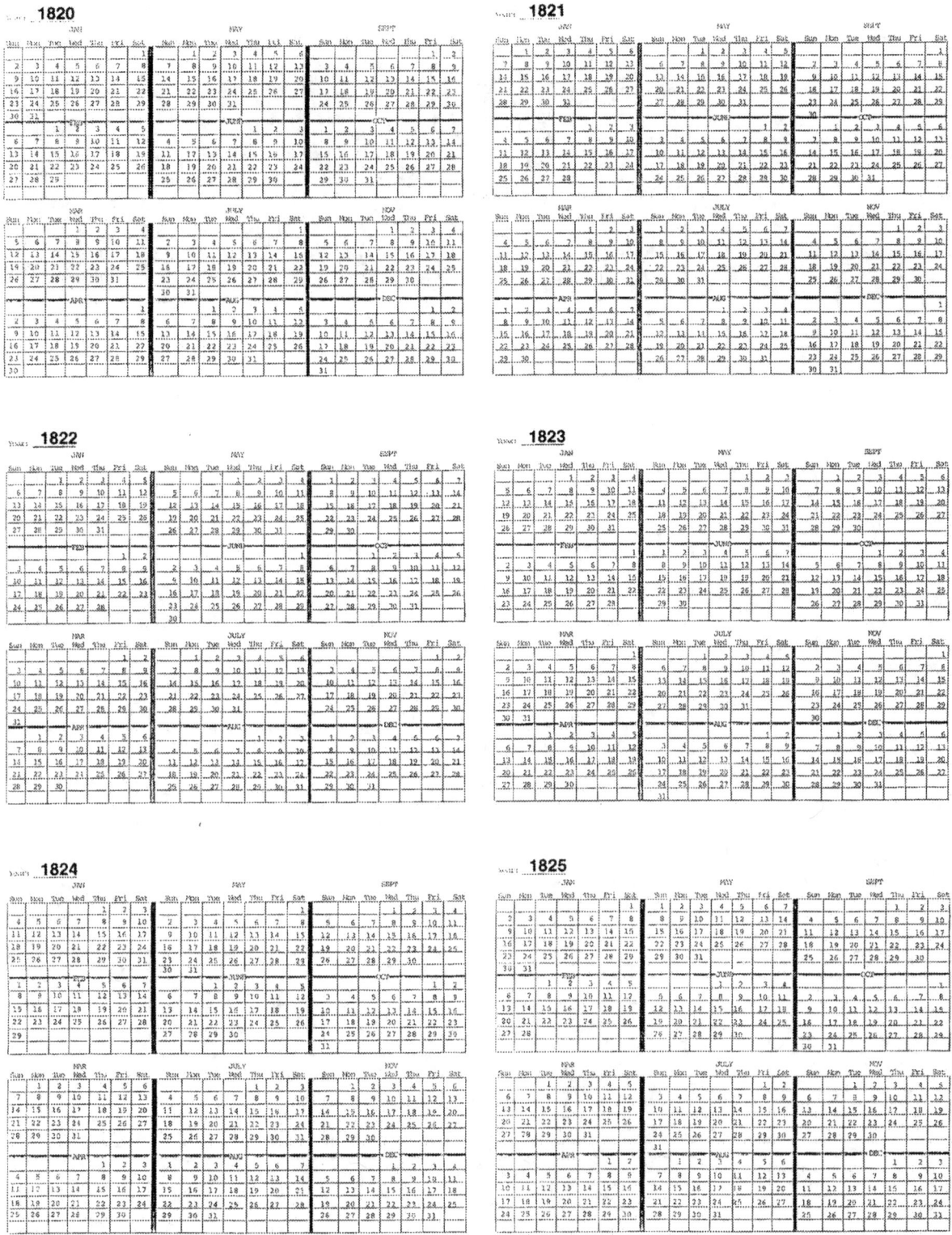

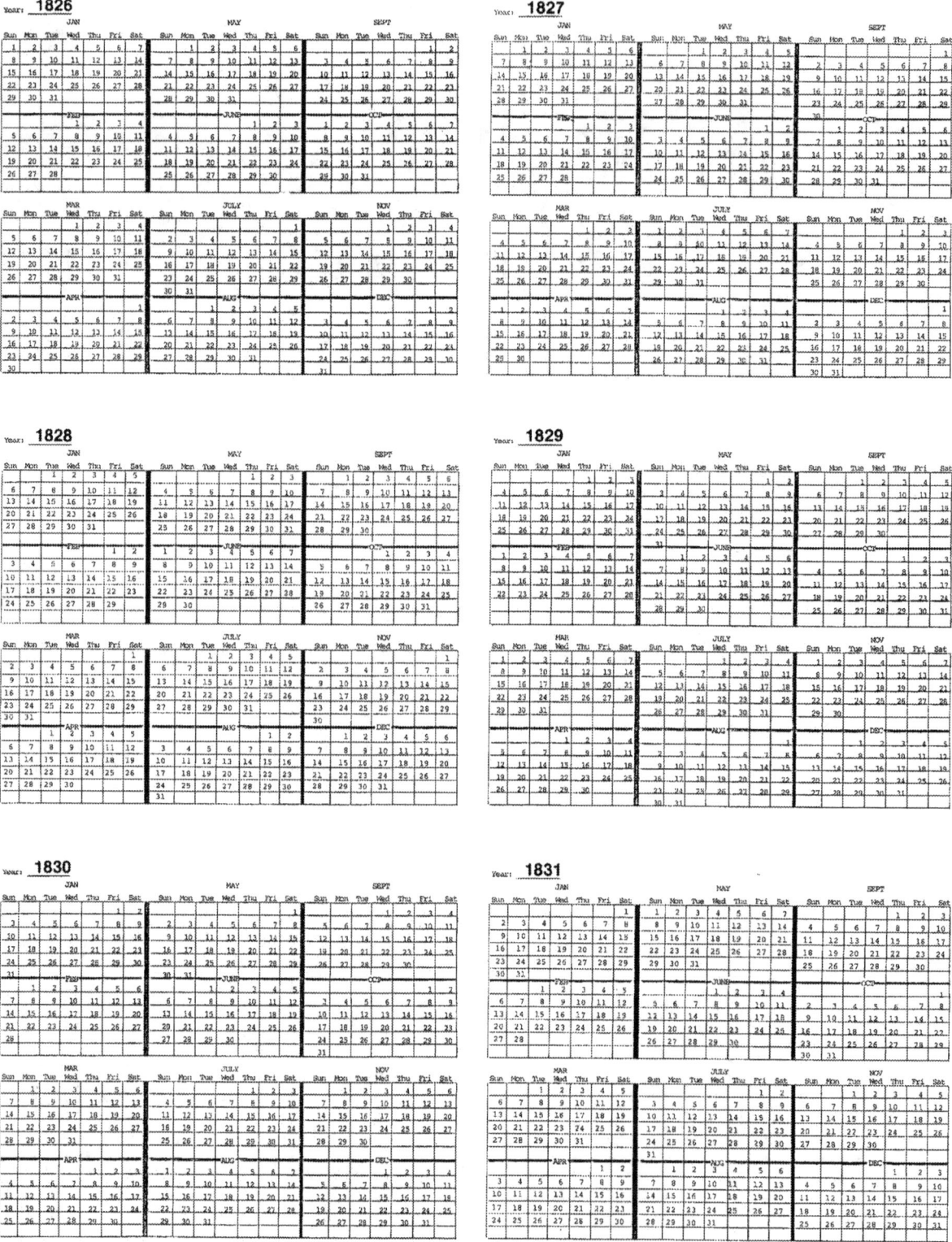

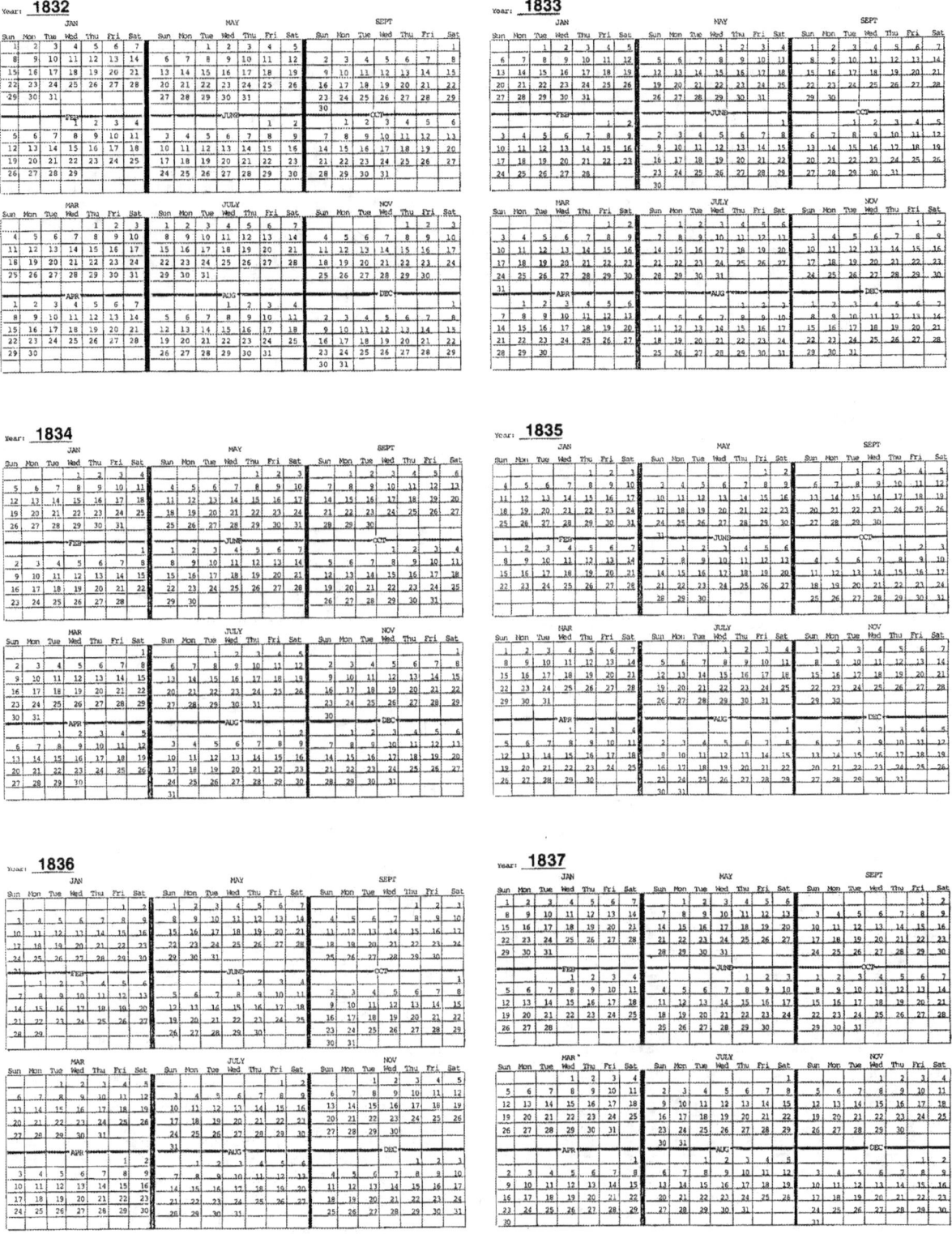

Year: 1838

JAN — MAY — SEPT

Sun	Mon	Tue	Wed	Thu	Fri	Sat

FEB — JUNE — OCT

MAR — JULY — NOV

APR — AUG — DEC

Year: 1839

JAN — MAY — SEPT

FEB — JUNE — OCT

MAR — JULY — NOV

APR — AUG — DEC

Year: 1840

JAN — MAY — SEPT

FEB — JUNE — OCT

MAR — JULY — NOV

APR — AUG — DEC

Year: 1841

JAN — MAY — SEPT

FEB — JUNE — OCT

MAR — JULY — NOV

APR — AUG — DEC

Year: 1842

JAN — MAY — SEPT

FEB — JUNE — OCT

MAR — JULY — NOV

APR — AUG — DEC

Year: 1843

JAN — MAY — SEPT

FEB — JUNE — OCT

MAR — JULY — NOV

APR — AUG — DEC

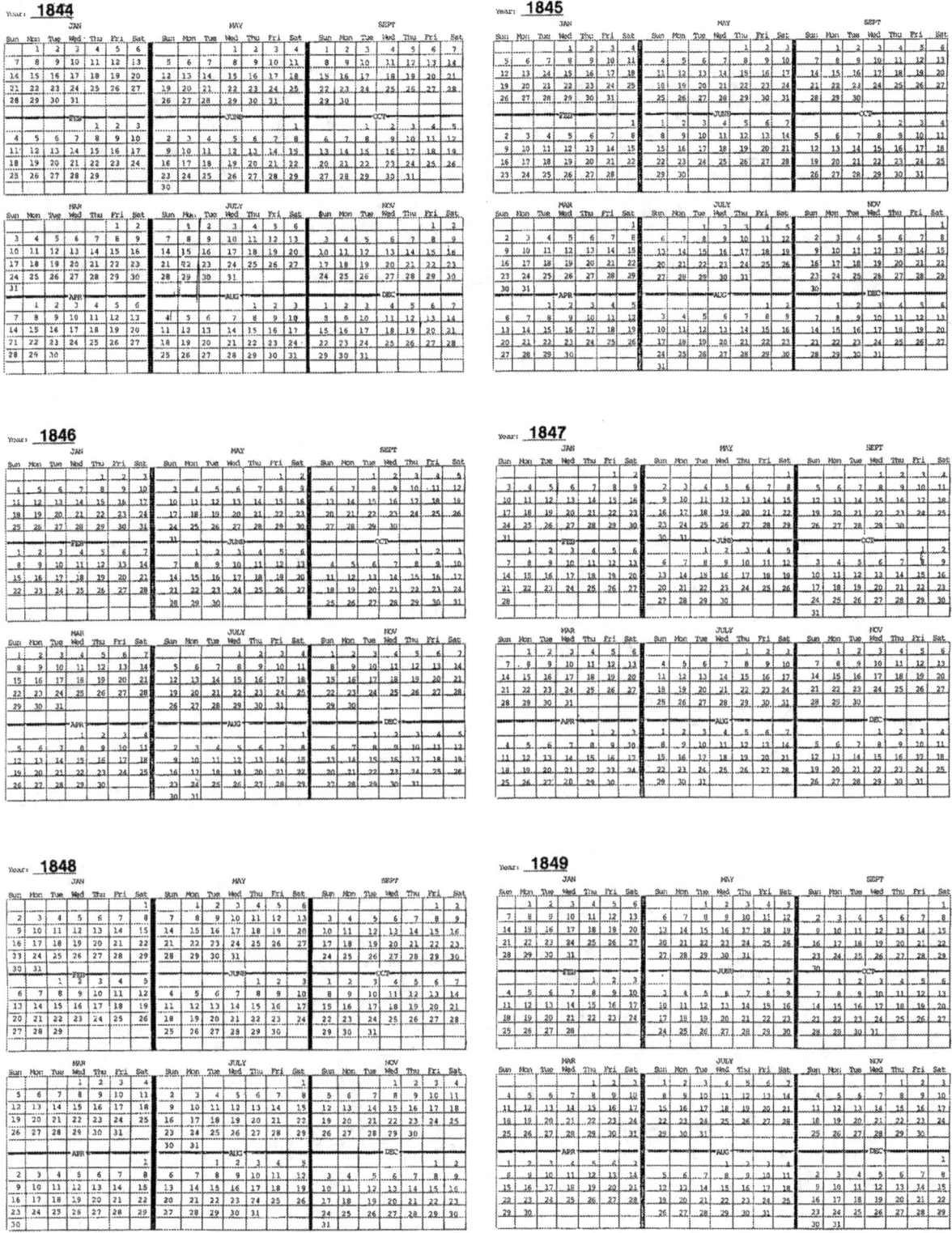

JAN MAY SEPT
FEB JUNE OCT
MAR JULY NOV
APR AUG DEC

JAN MAY SEPT
FEB JUNE OCT
MAR JULY NOV
APR AUG DEC

JAN MAY SEPT
FEB JUNE OCT
MAR JULY NOV
APR AUG DEC

JAN MAY SEPT
FEB JUNE OCT
MAR JULY NOV
APR AUG DEC

JAN MAY SEPT
FEB JUNE OCT
MAR JULY NOV
APR AUG DEC

JAN MAY SEPT
FEB JUNE OCT
MAR JULY NOV
APR AUG DEC

18

Year: **1856**

Year: **1857**

Year: **1858**

Year: **1859**

Year: **1860**

Year: **1861**

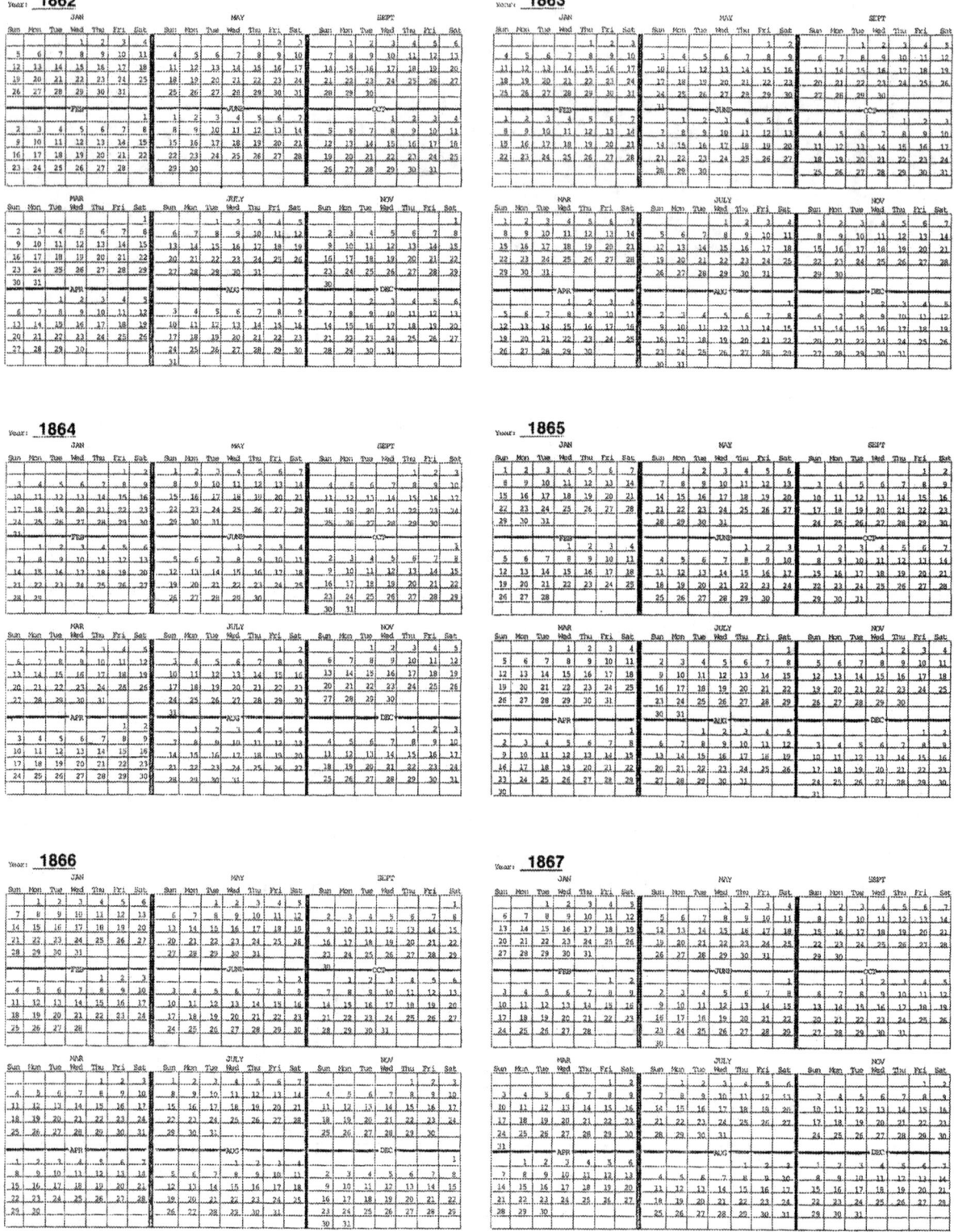

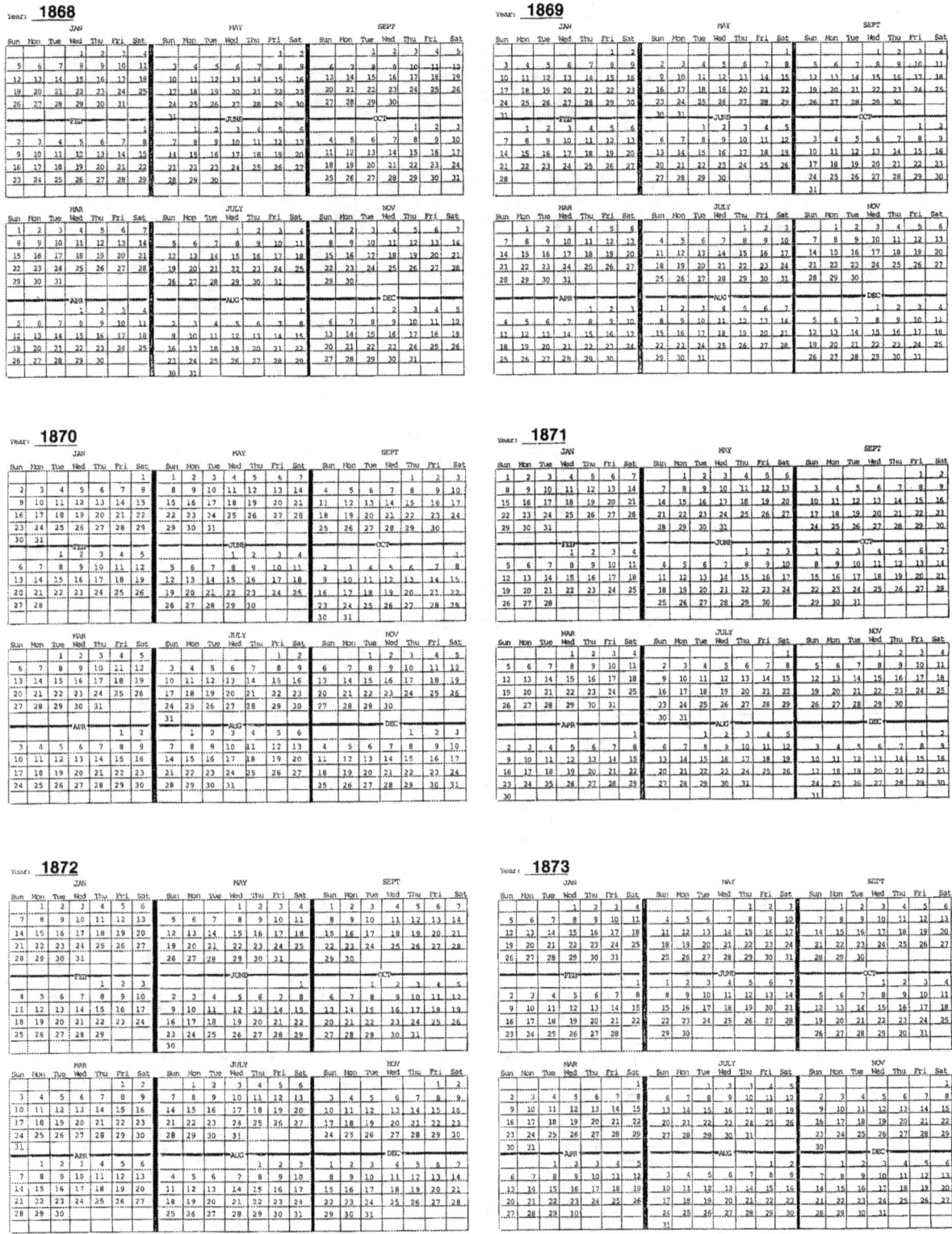

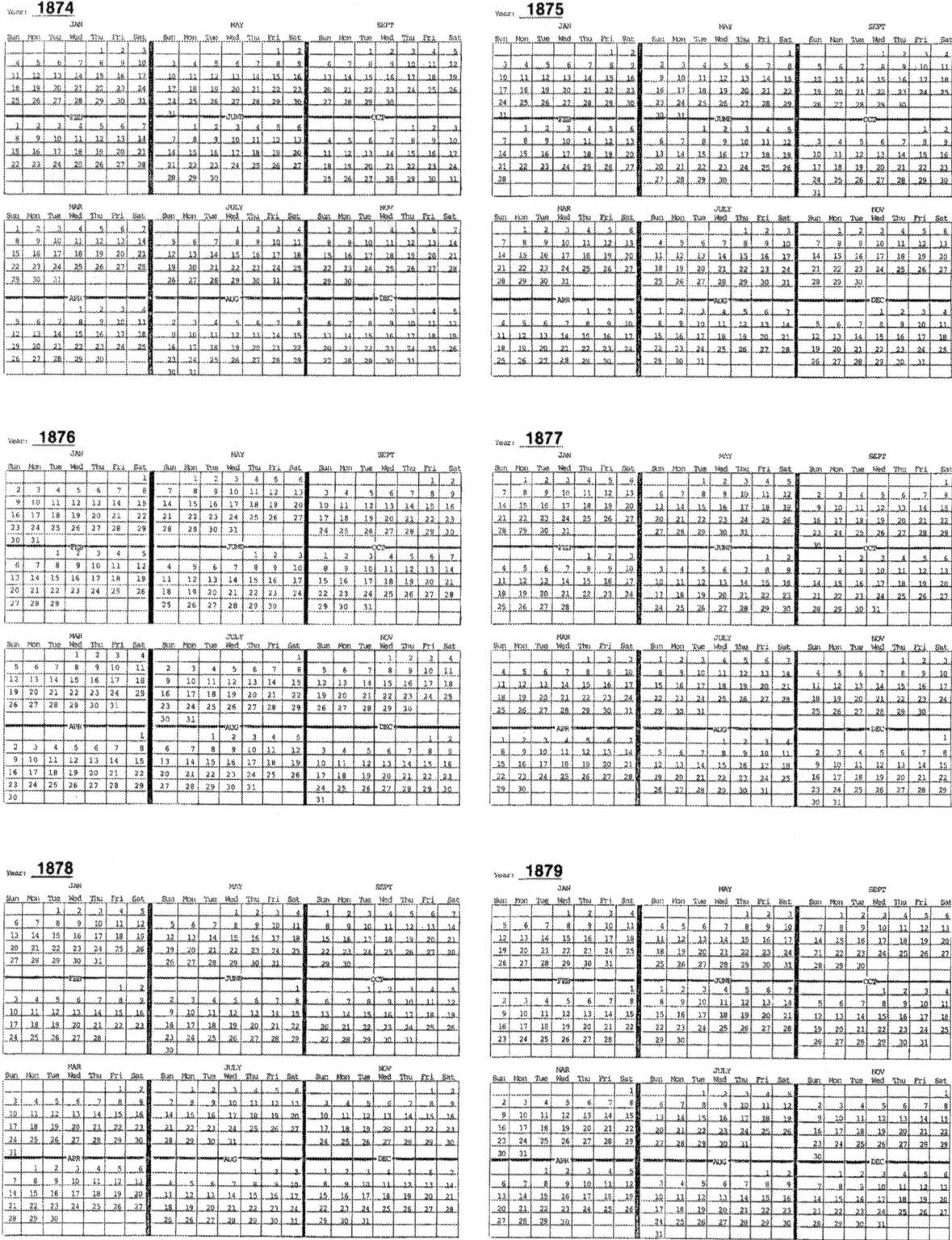

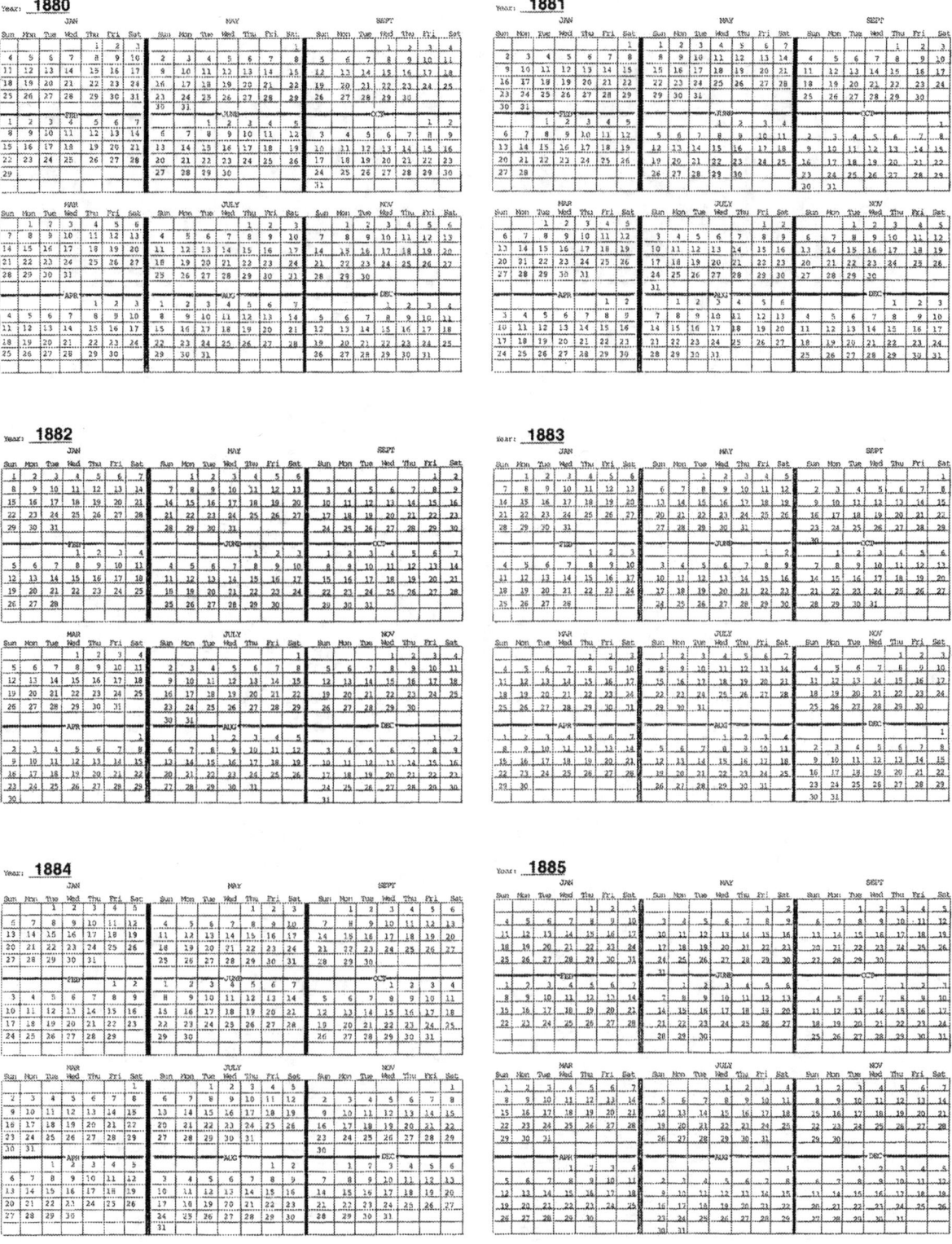

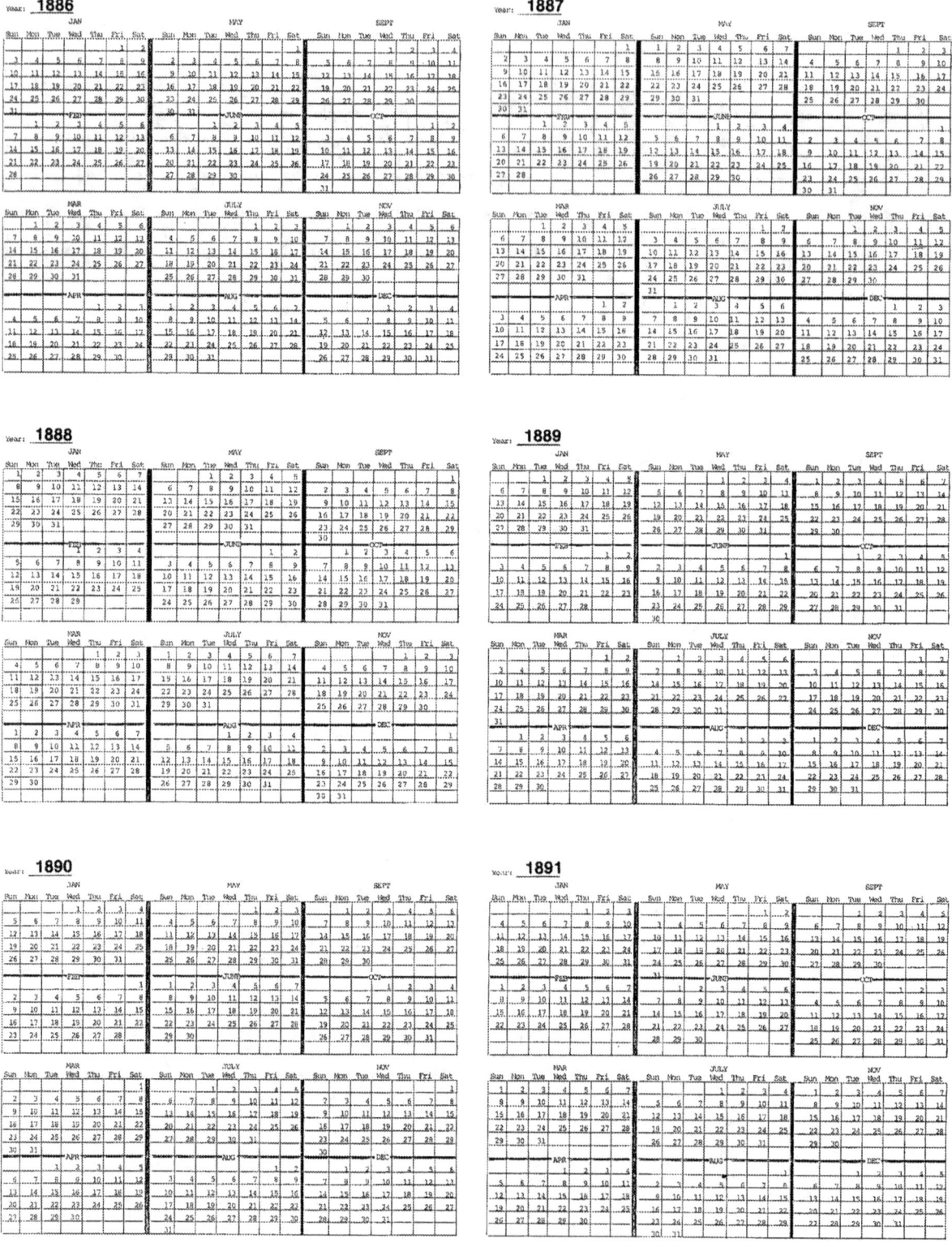

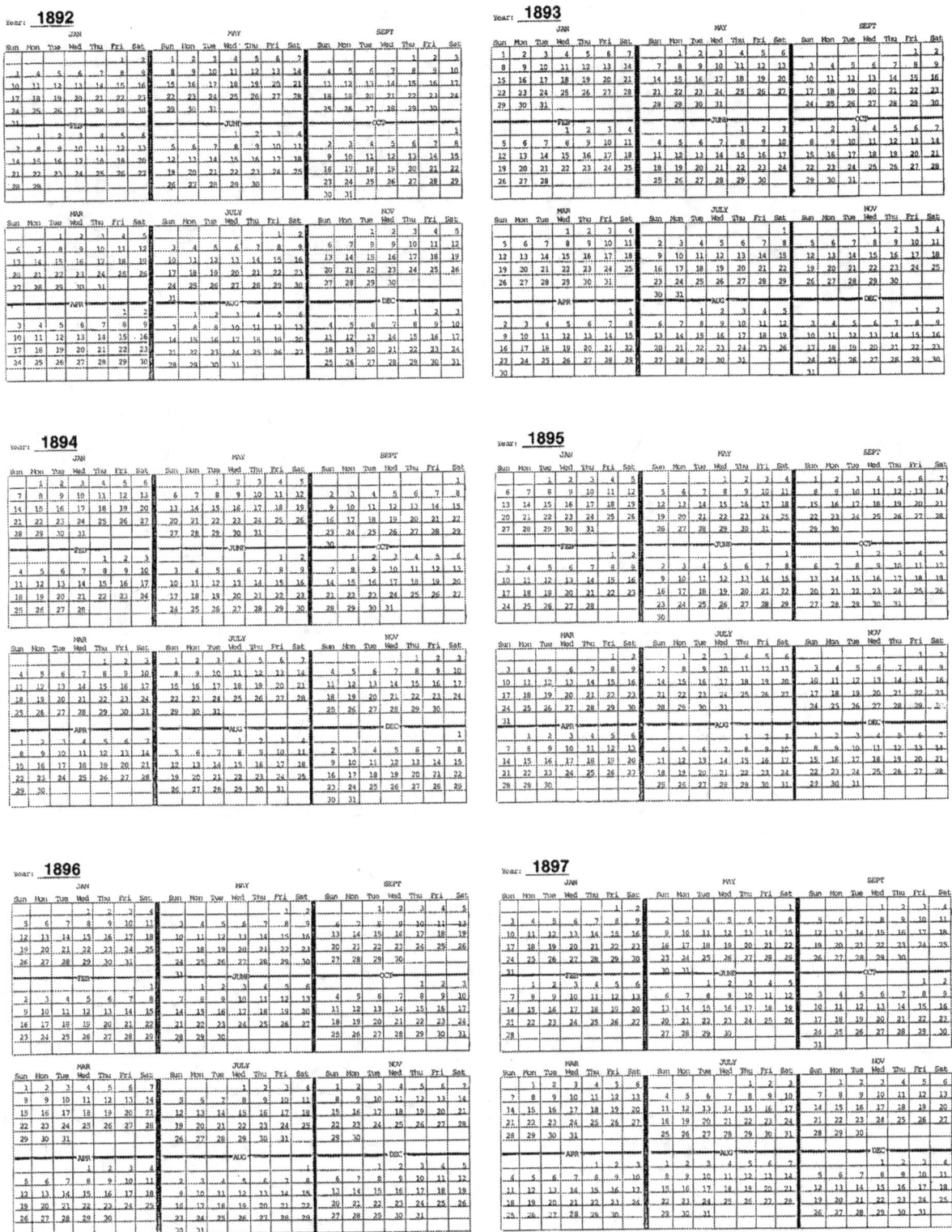

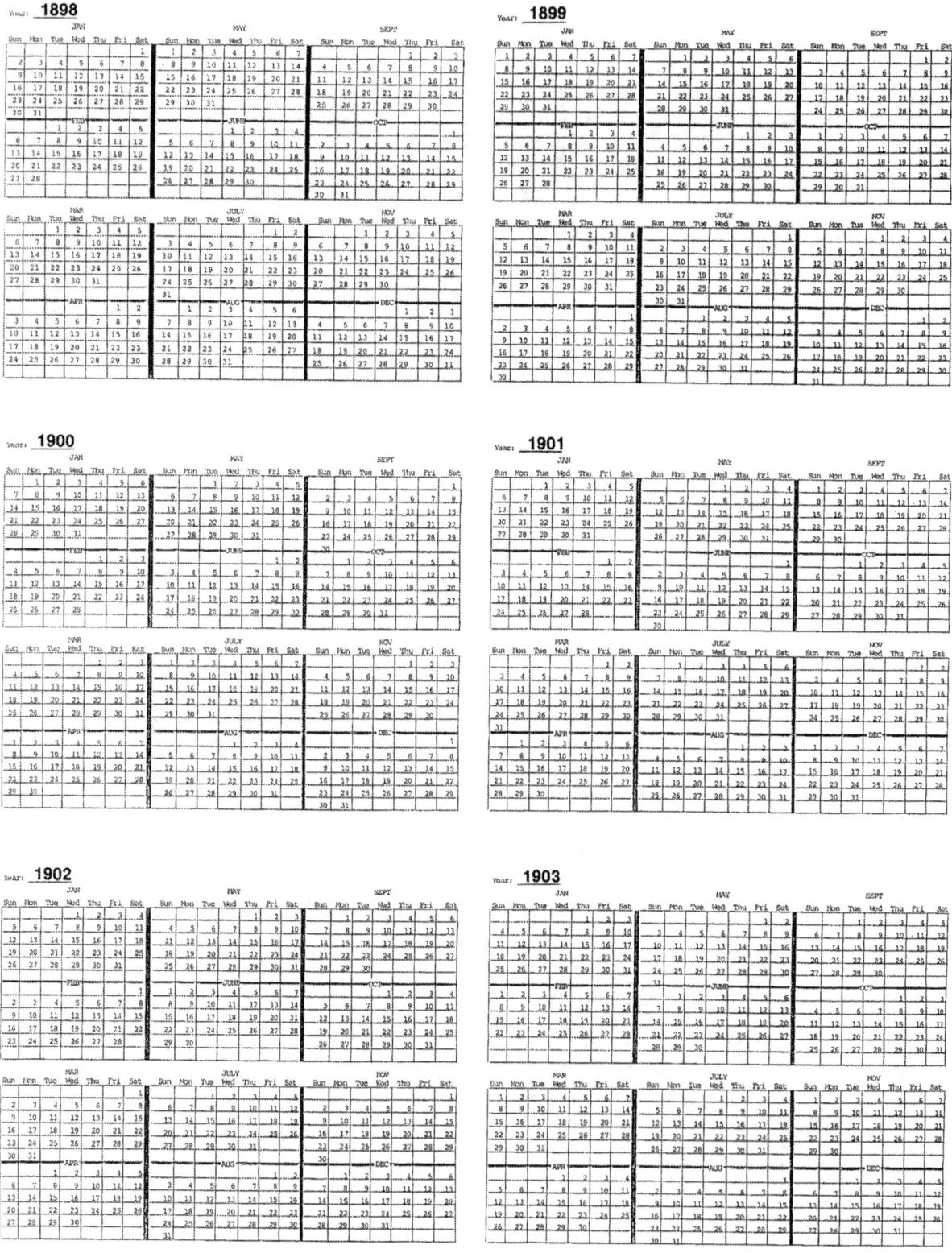

Year: **1898**

Year: **1899**

Year: **1900**

Year: **1901**

Year: **1902**

Year: **1903**

26

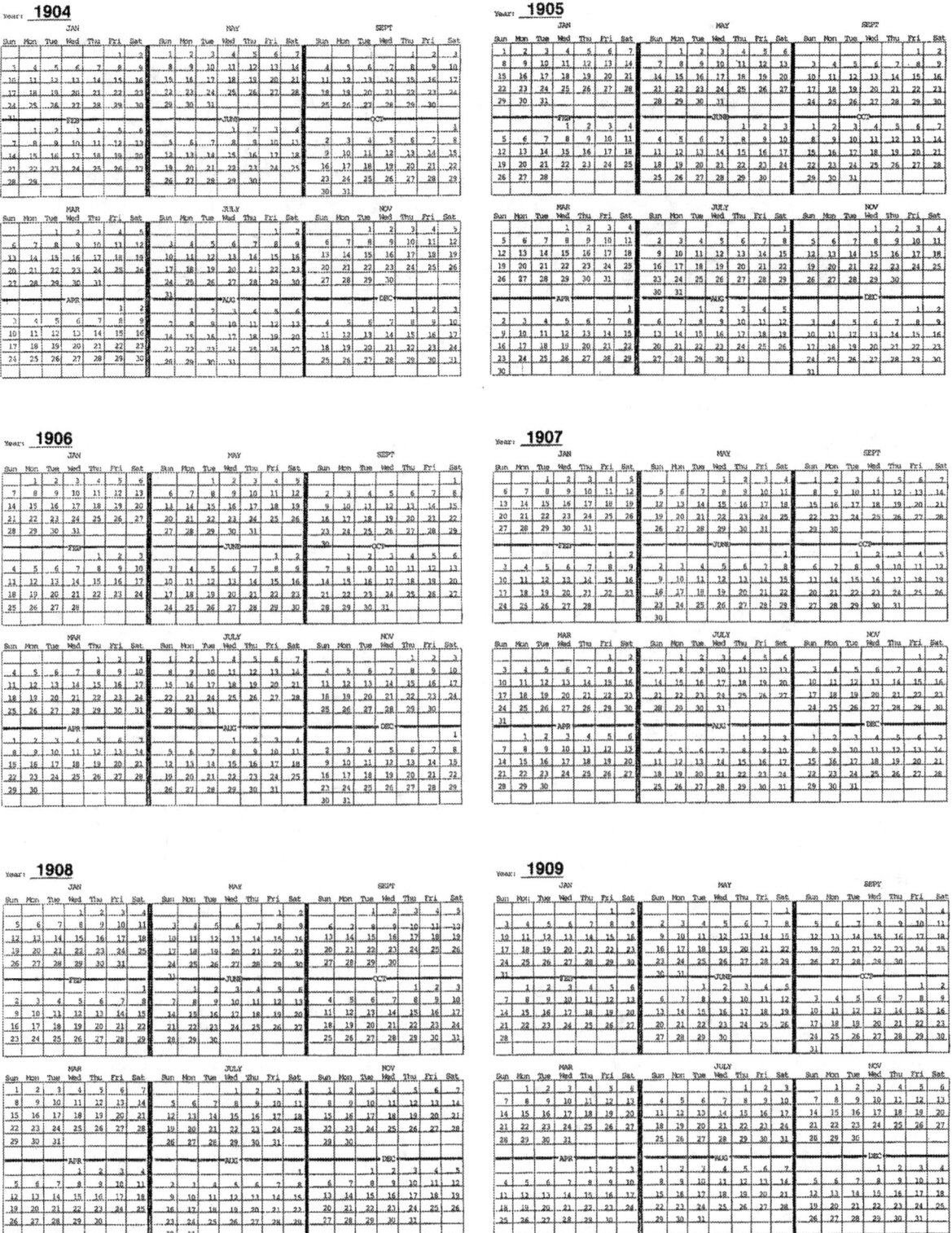

JAN   MAY   SEPT

Sun	Mon	Tue	Wed	Thu	Fri	Sat

FEB   JUNE   OCT

MAR   JULY   NOV

APR   AUG   DEC

Year: **1911**

JAN   MAY   SEPT

FEB   JUNE   OCT

MAR   JULY   NOV

APR   AUG   DEC

Year: **1912**

JAN   MAY   SEPT

FEB   JUNE   OCT

MAR   JULY   NOV

APR   AUG   DEC

Year: **1913**

JAN   MAY   SEPT

FEB   JUNE   OCT

MAR   JULY   NOV

APR   AUG   DEC

Year: **1914**

JAN   MAY   SEPT

FEB   JUNE   OCT

MAR   JULY   NOV

APR   AUG   DEC

Year: **1915**

JAN   MAY   SEPT

FEB   JUNE   OCT

MAR   JULY   NOV

APR   AUG   DEC

Year: **1916**

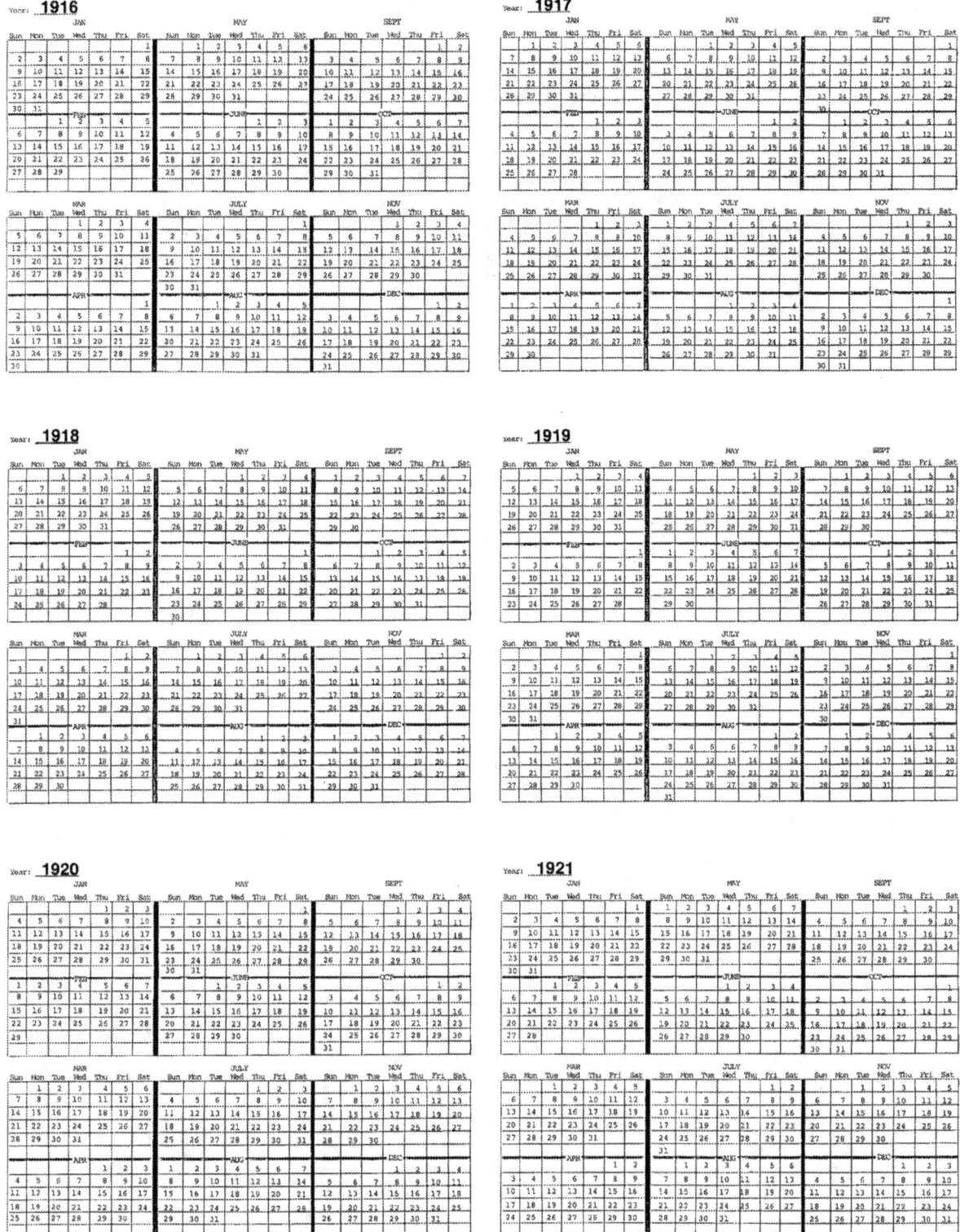

Year: **1917**

Year: **1918**

Year: **1919**

Year: **1920**

Year: **1921**

JAN   MAY   SEPT

Sun	Mon	Tue	Wed	Thu	Fri	Sat
1	2	3	4	5	6	7
8	9	10	11	12	13	14
15	16	17	18	19	20	21
22	23	24	25	26	27	28
29	30	31				

30

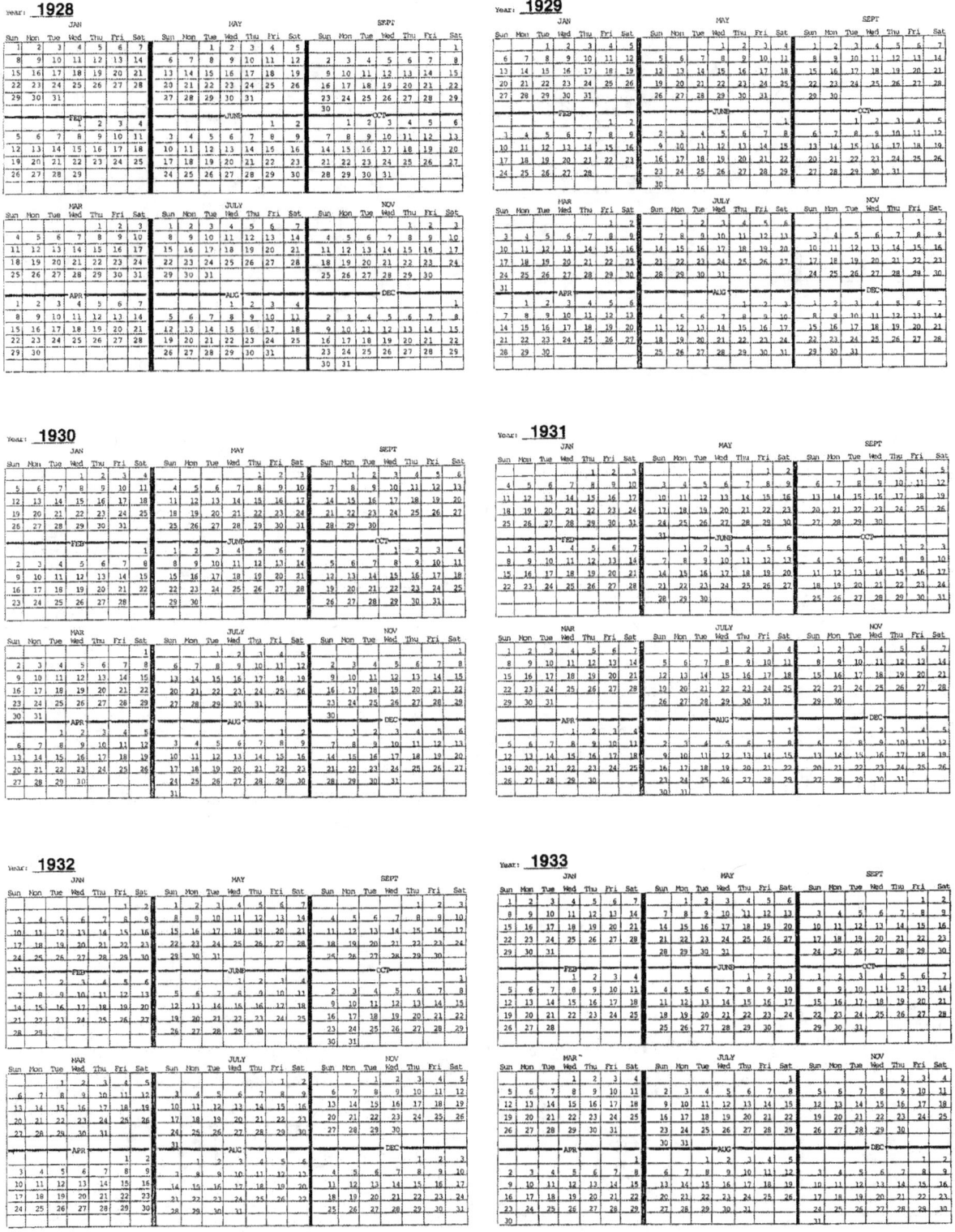

31

Year: **1934**

Year: **1935**

Year: **1936**

Year: **1937**

Year: **1938**

Year: **1939**

32

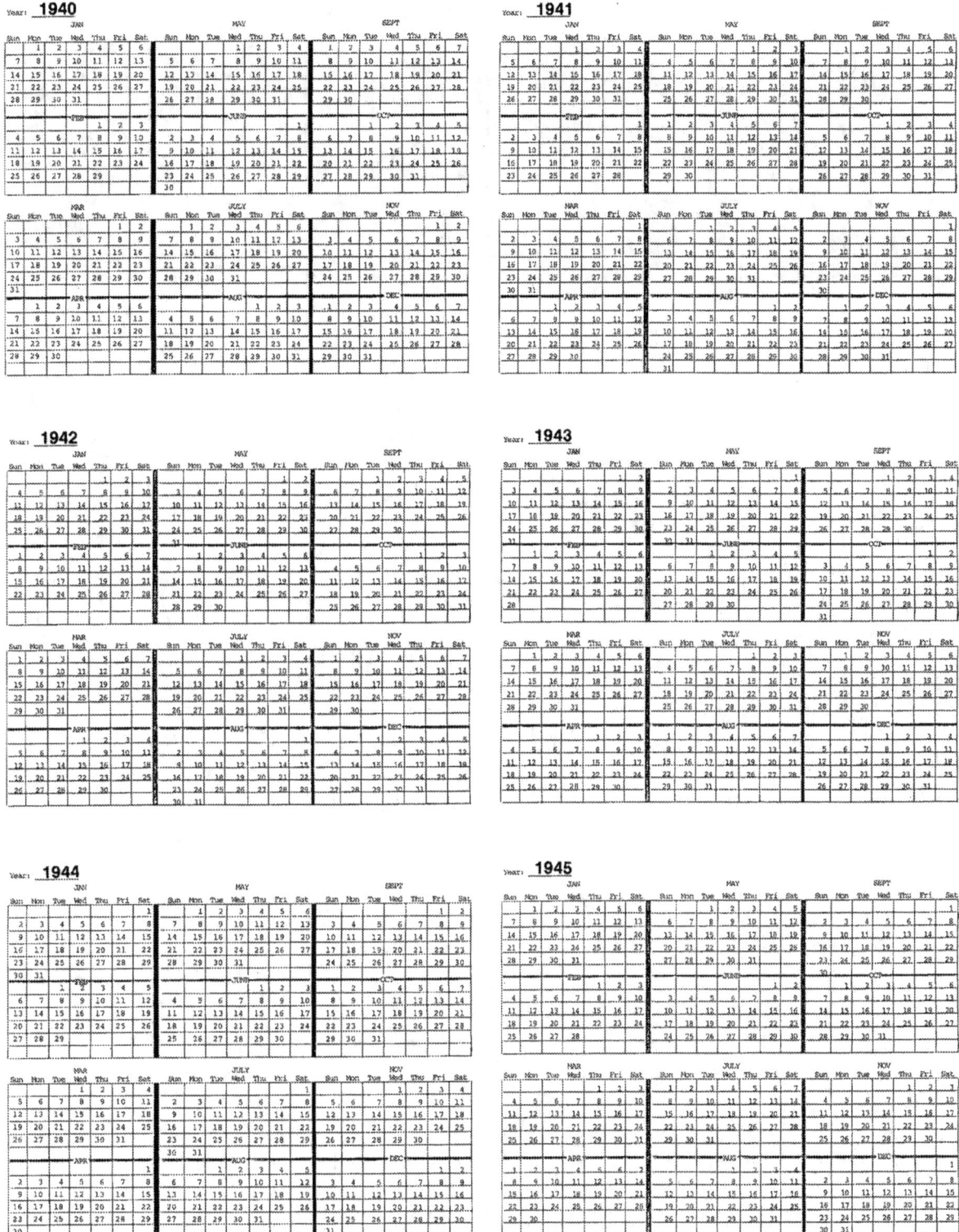

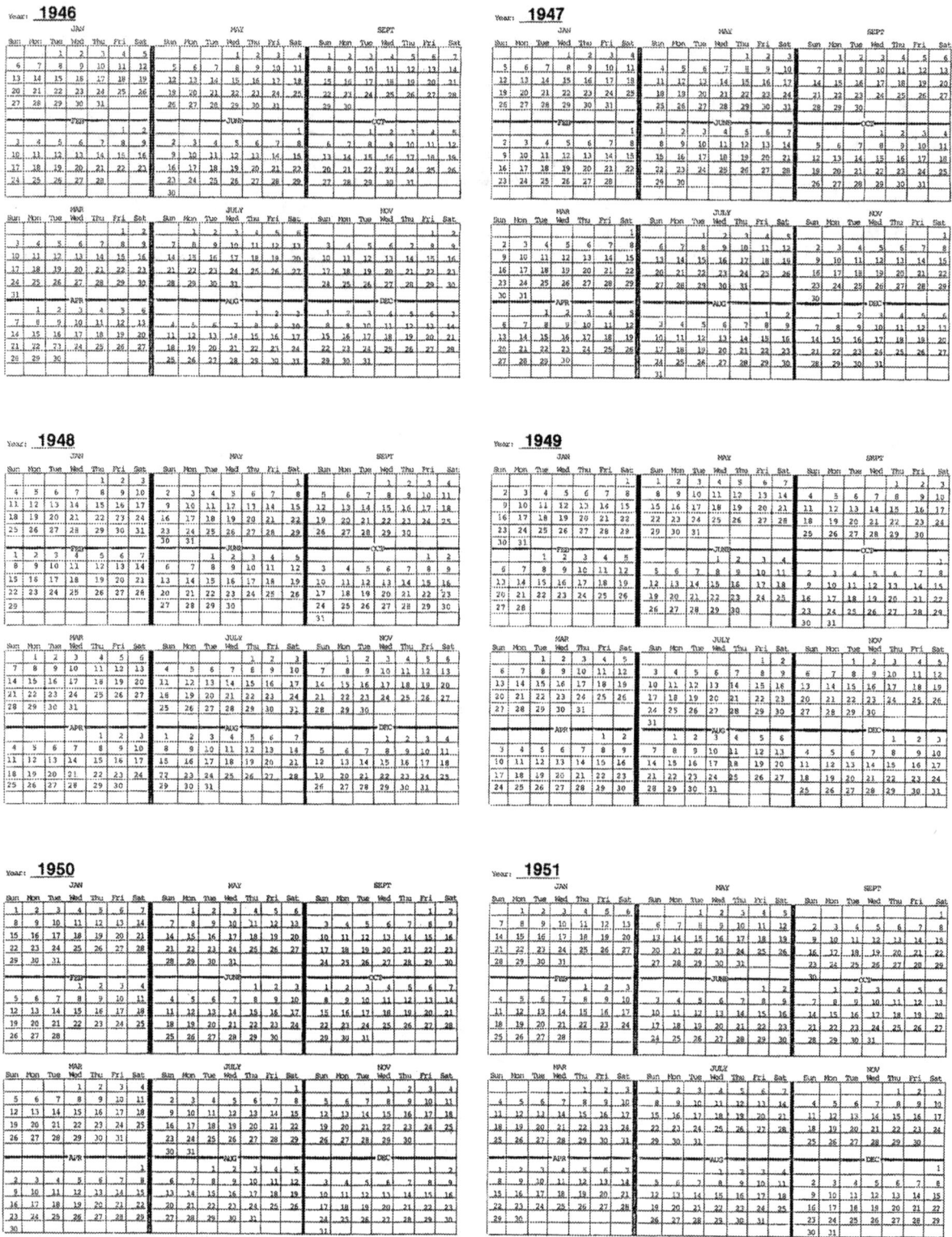

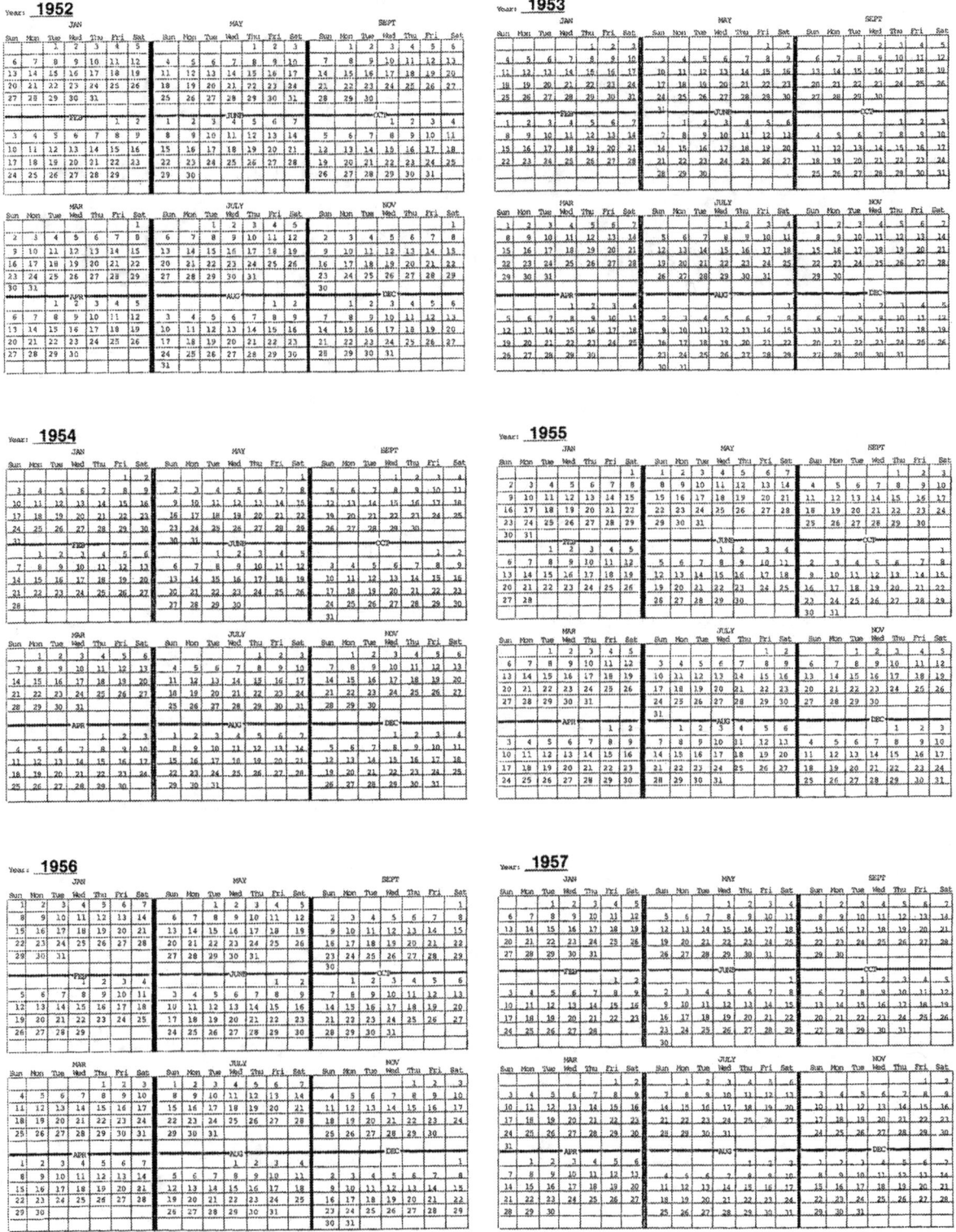

JAN | MAY | SEPT
Sun Mon Tue Wed Thu Fri Sat

FEB | JUNE | OCT

MAR | JULY | NOV

APR | AUG | DEC

Year: **1959**

JAN | MAY | SEPT
Sun Mon Tue Wed Thu Fri Sat

FEB | JUNE | OCT

MAR | JULY | NOV

APR | AUG | DEC

Year: **1960**

JAN | MAY | SEPT
Sun Mon Tue Wed Thu Fri Sat

FEB | JUNE | OCT

MAR | JULY | NOV

APR | AUG | DEC

Year: **1961**

JAN | MAY | SEPT
Sun Mon Tue Wed Thu Fri Sat

FEB | JUNE | OCT

MAR | JULY | NOV

APR | AUG | DEC

Year: **1962**

JAN | MAY | SEPT
Sun Mon Tue Wed Thu Fri Sat

FEB | JUNE | OCT

MAR | JULY | NOV

APR | AUG | DEC

Year: **1963**

JAN | MAY | SEPT
Sun Mon Tue Wed Thu Fri Sat

FEB | JUNE | OCT

MAR | JULY | NOV

APR | AUG | DEC

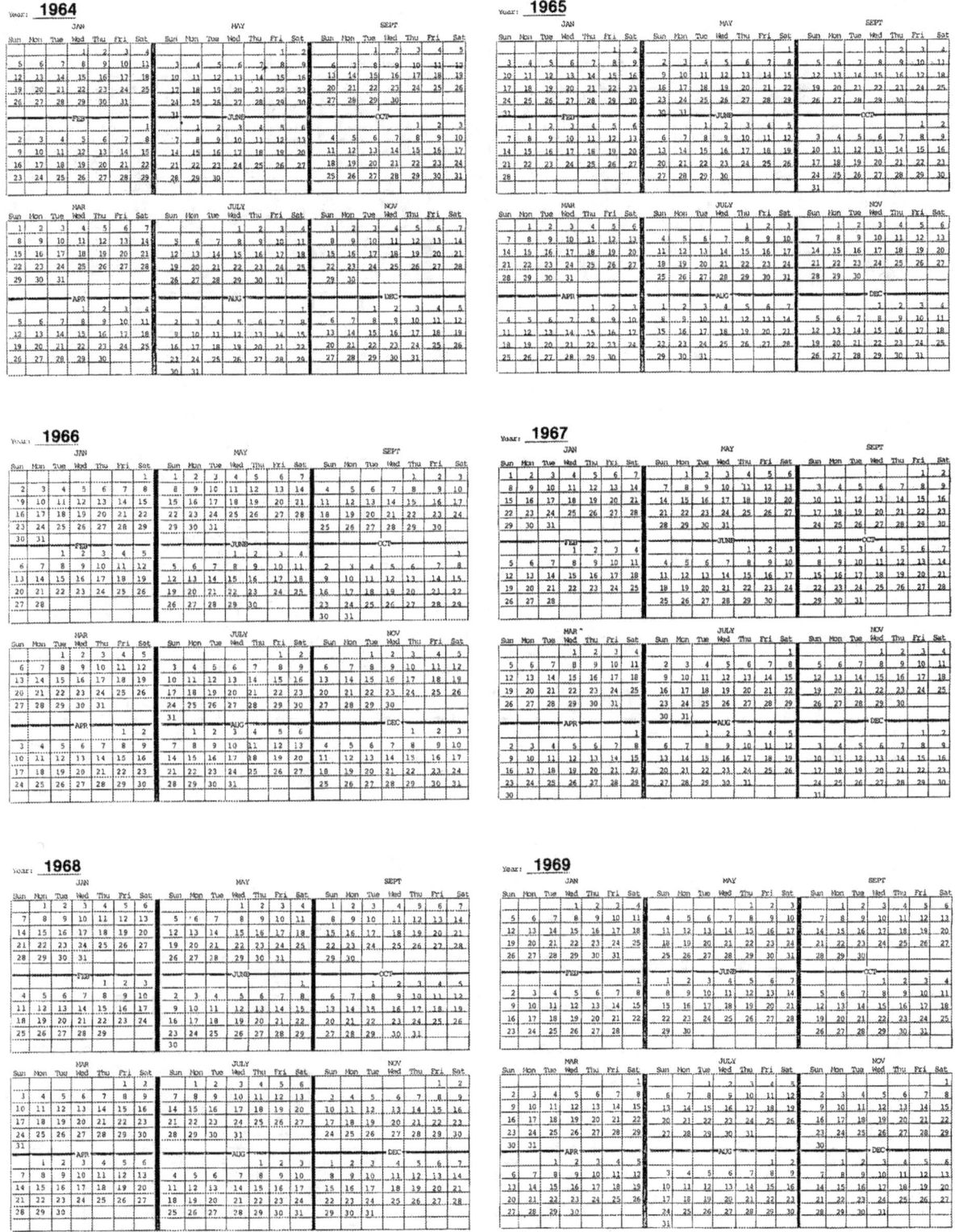

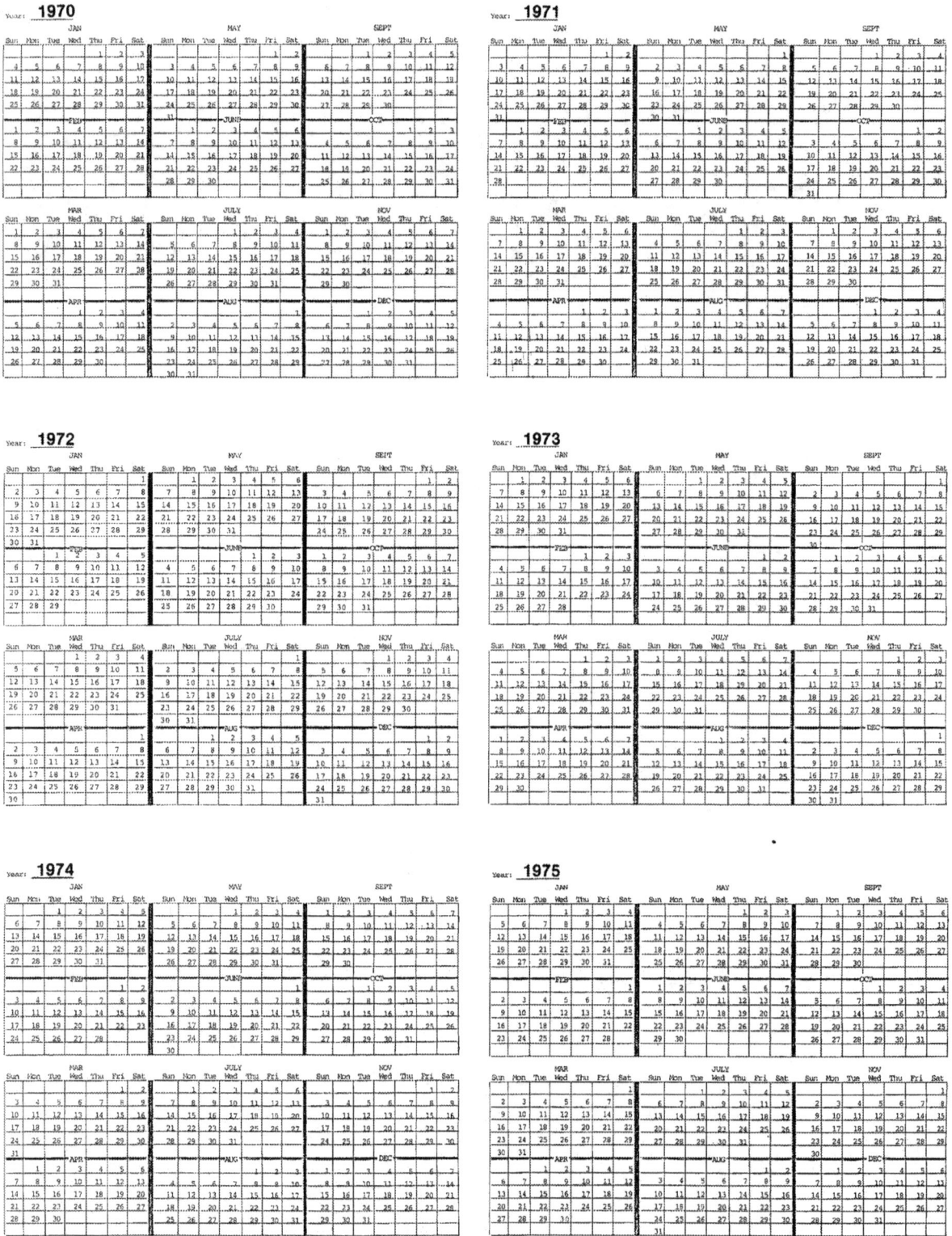

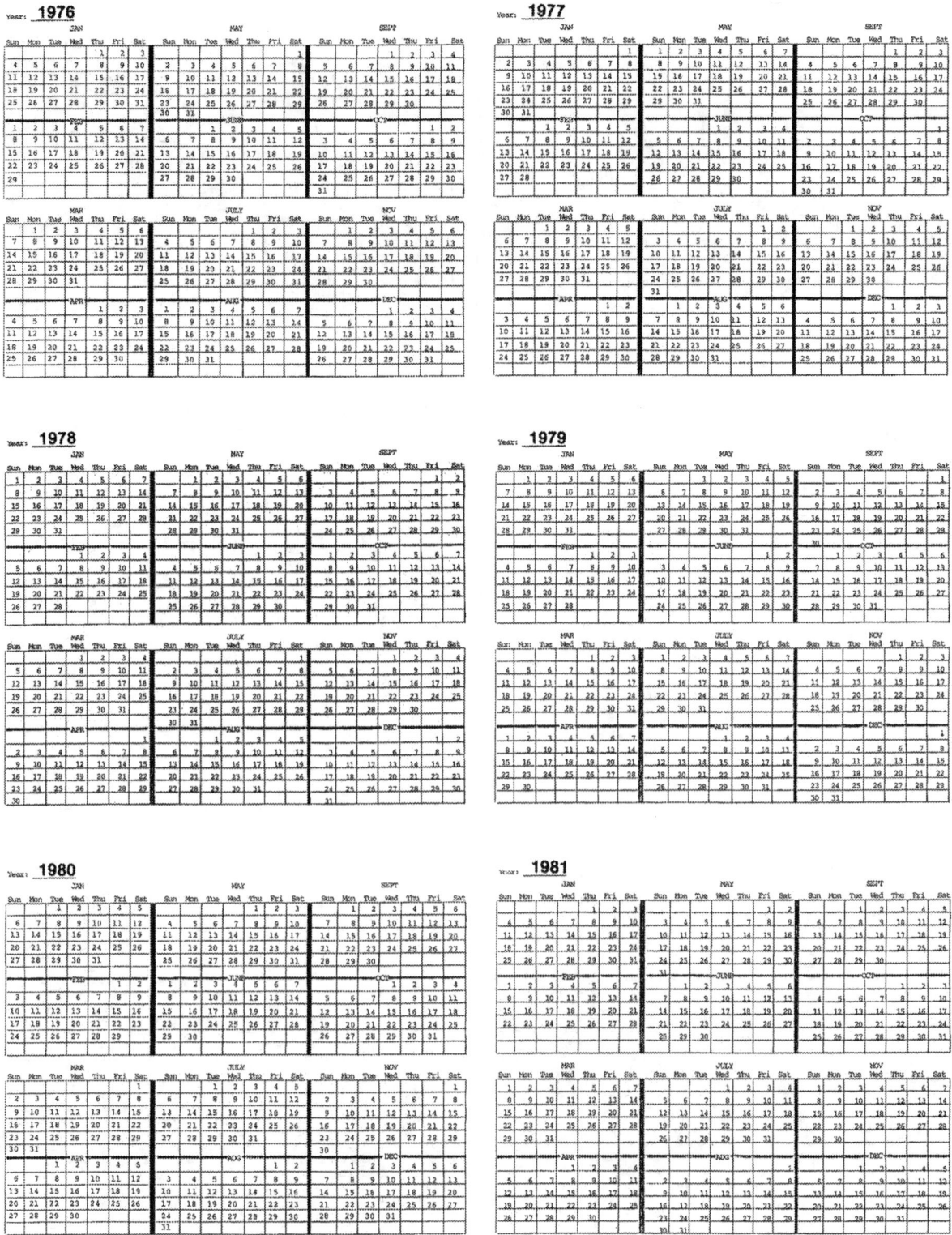

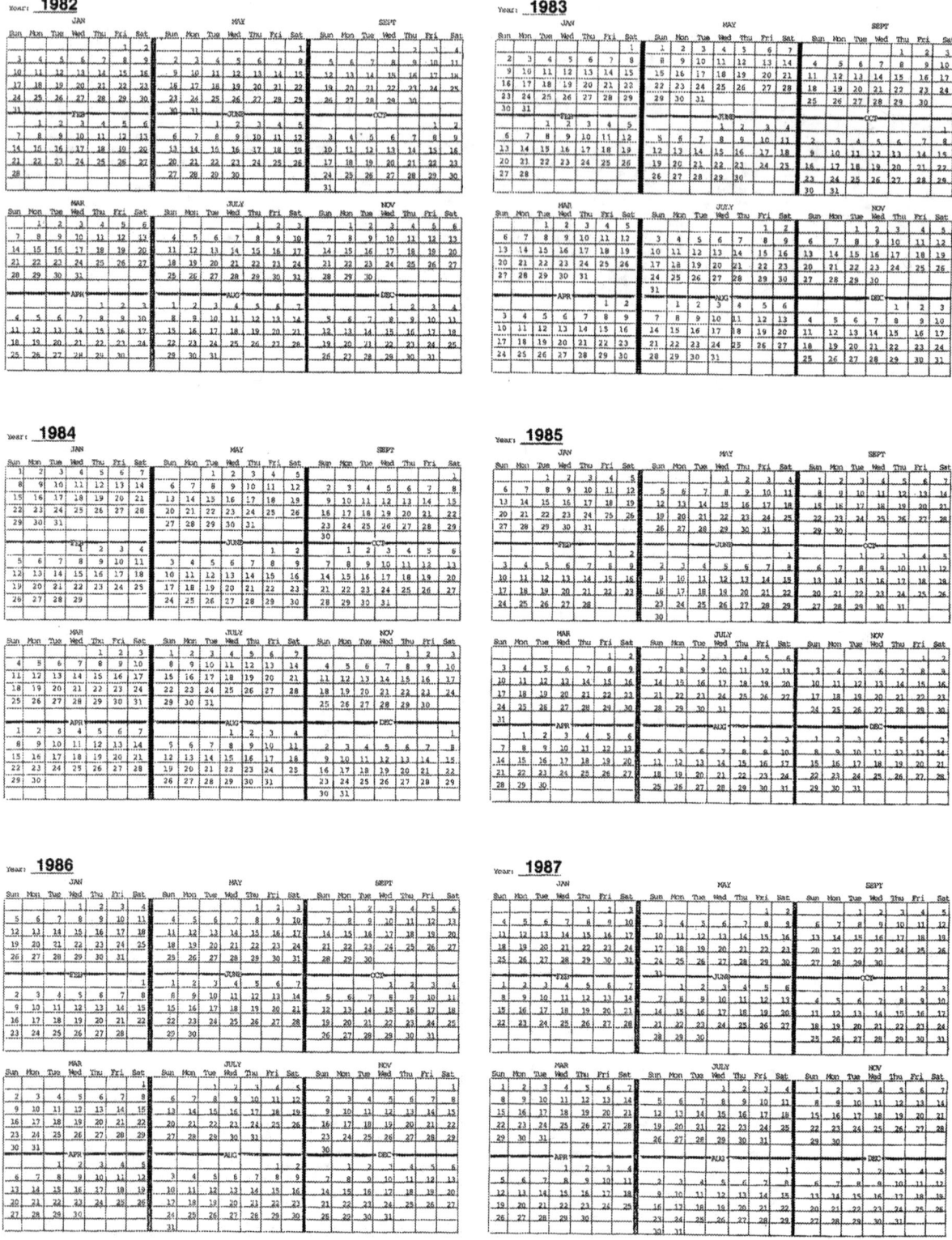

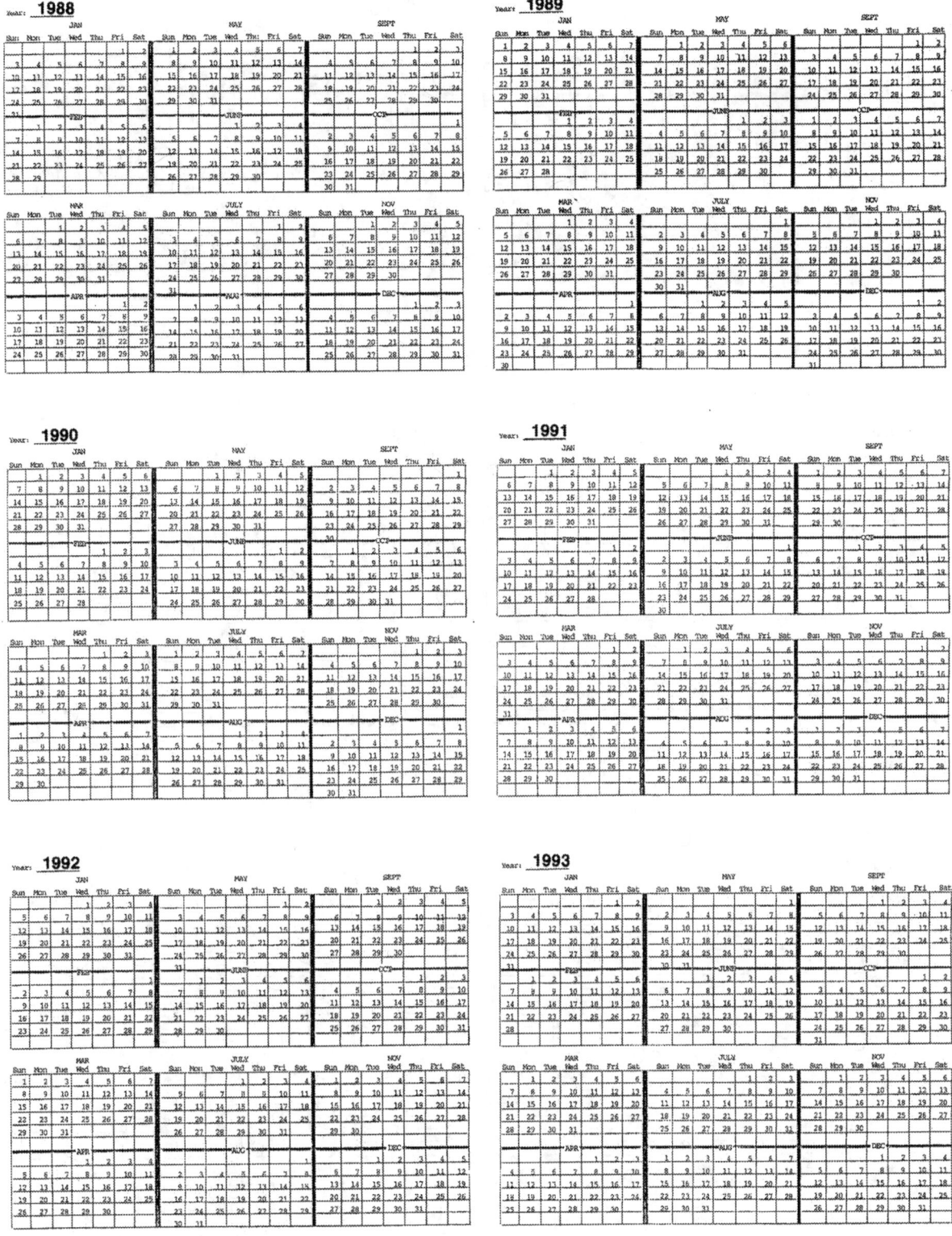

Year: **1994**

Year: **1995**

Year: **1996**

Year: **1997**

Year: **1998**

Year: **1999**

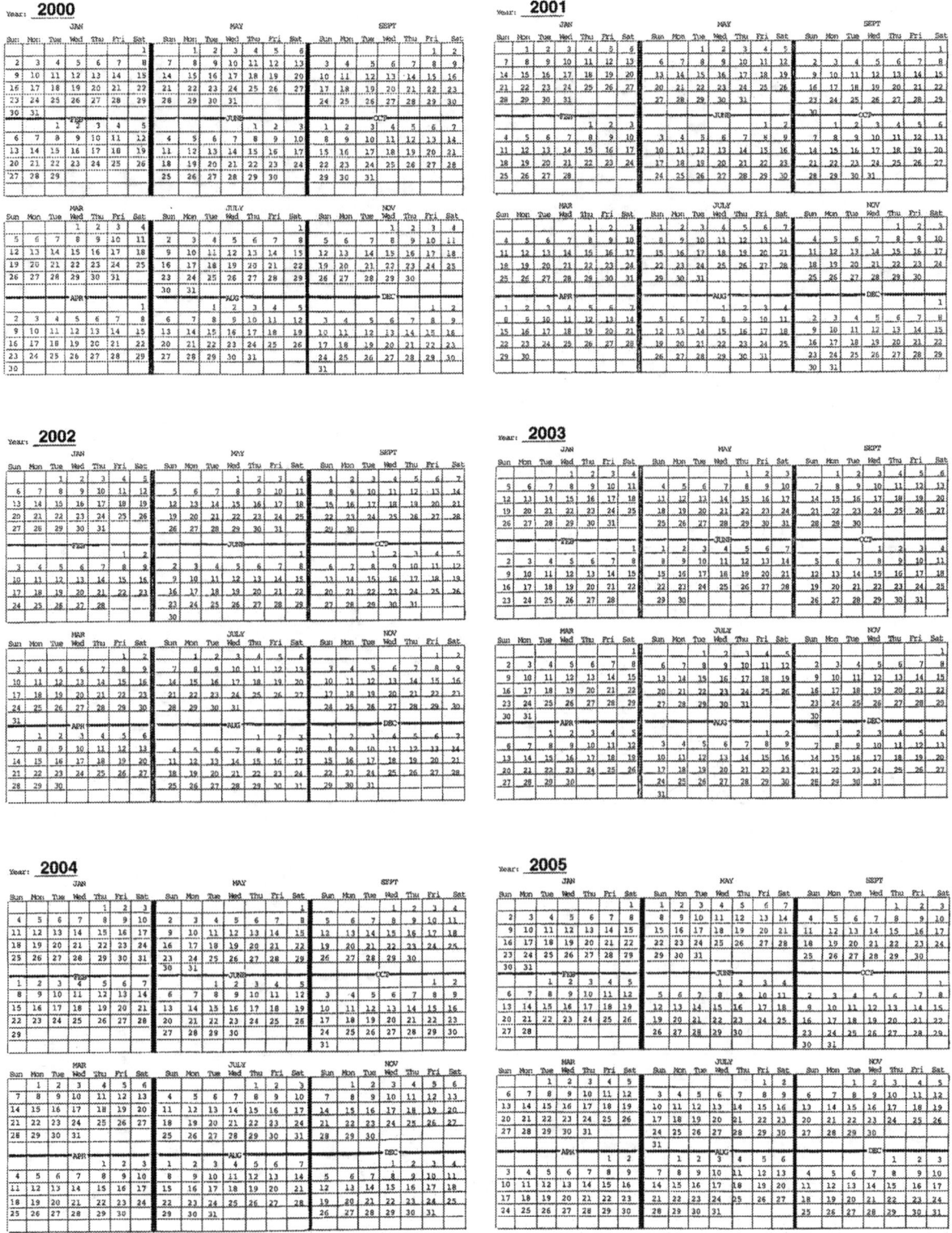

Year: **2006**

Year: **2007**

Year: **2008**

Year: **2009**

Year: **2010**

Year: **2011**

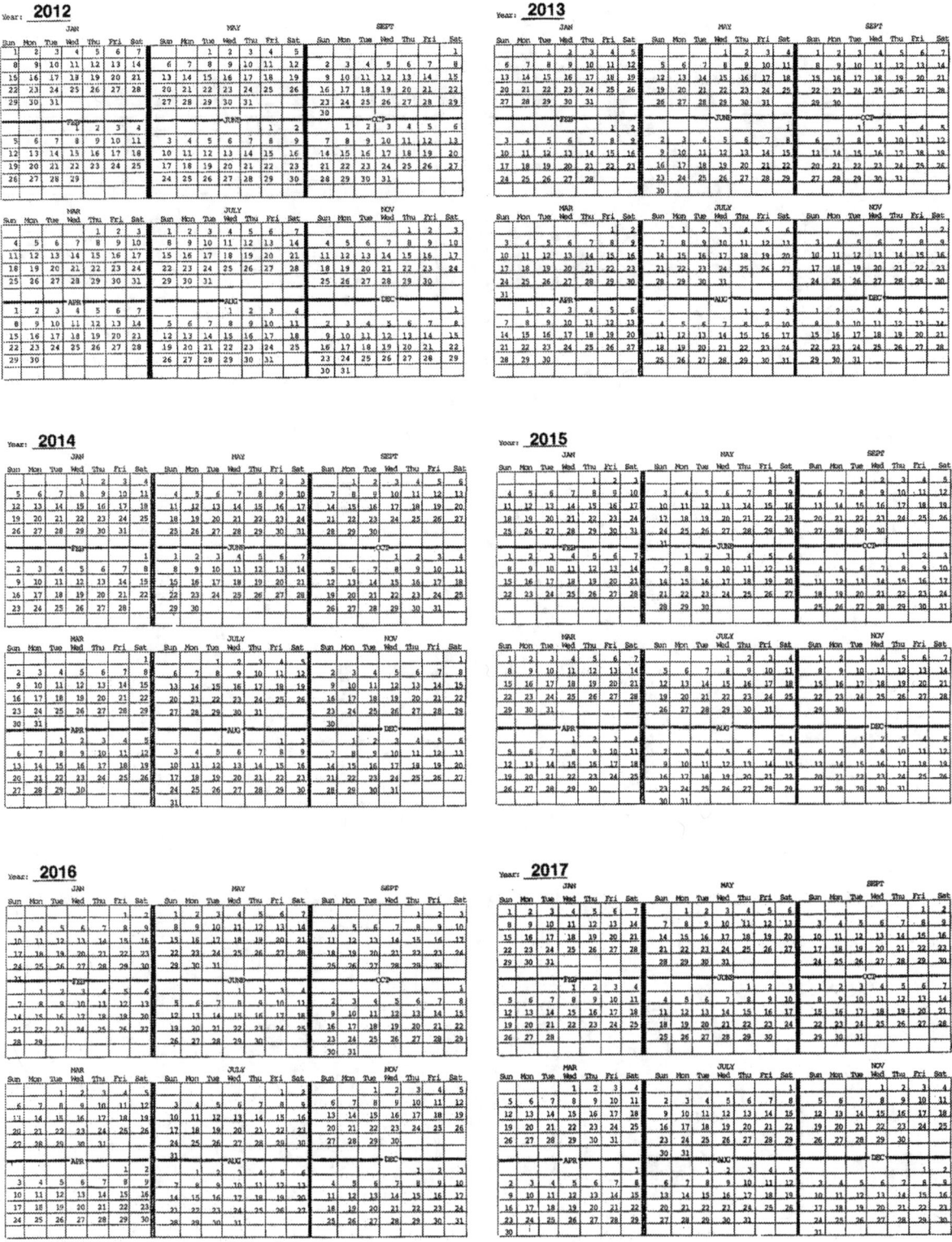

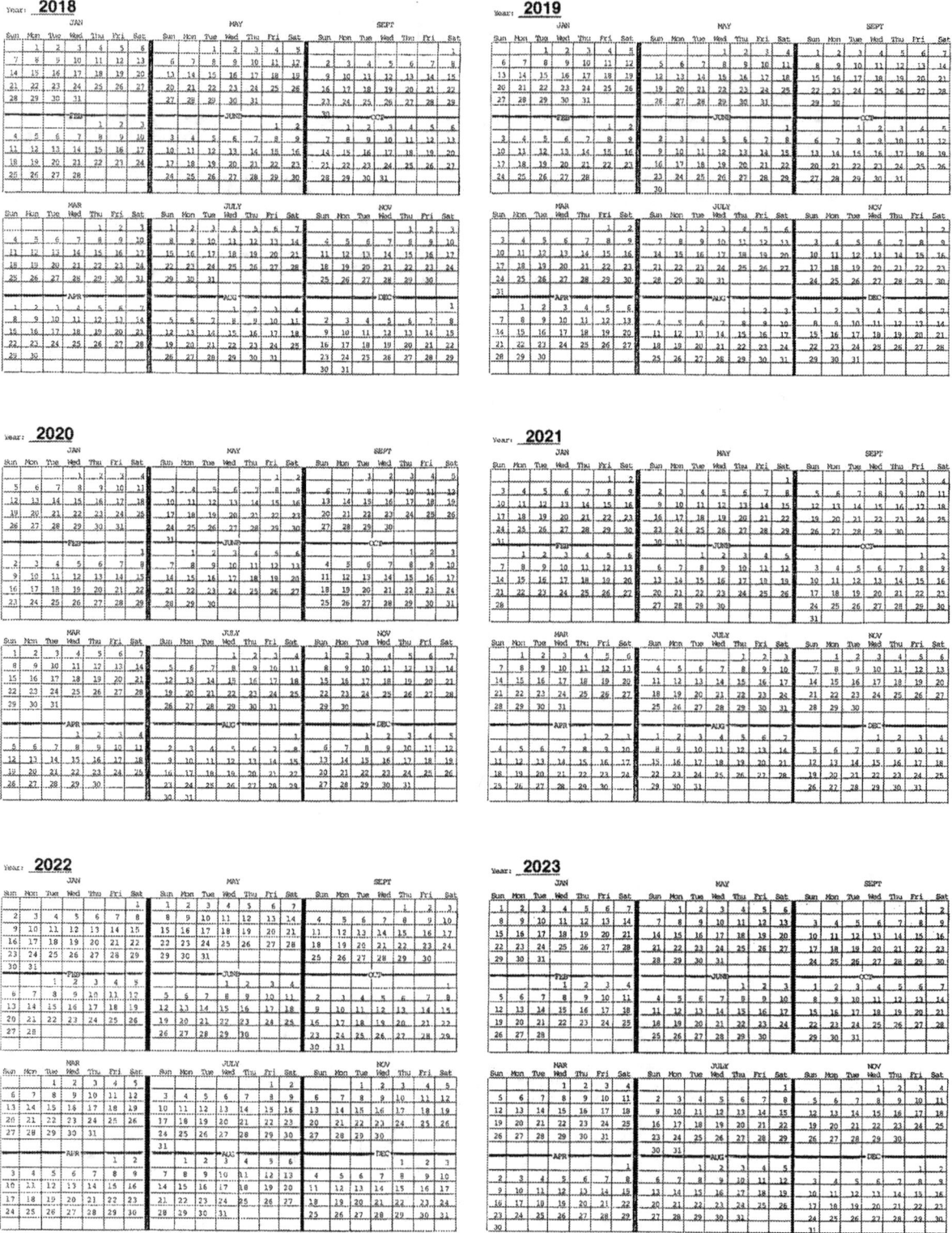

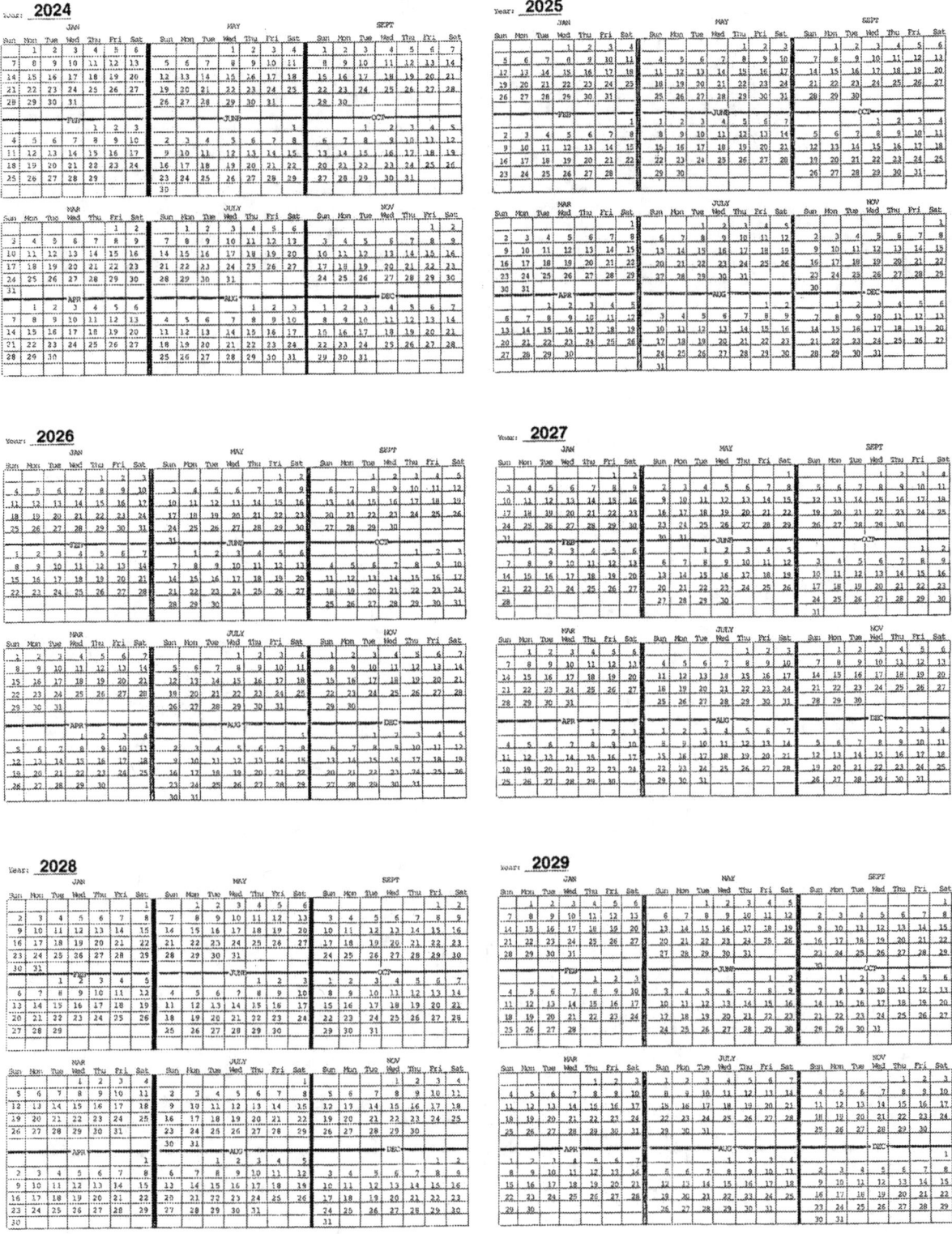

JAN · MAY · SEPT

Sun	Mon	Tue	Wed	Thu	Fri	Sat

FEB · JUNE · OCT

MAR · JULY · NOV

APR · AUG · DEC

JAN · MAY · SEPT

FEB · JUNE · OCT

MAR · JULY · NOV

APR · AUG · DEC

JAN · MAY · SEPT

FEB · JUNE · OCT

MAR · JULY · NOV

APR · AUG · DEC

JAN · MAY · SEPT

FEB · JUNE · OCT

MAR · JULY · NOV

APR · AUG · DEC

JAN · MAY · SEPT

FEB · JUNE · OCT

MAR · JULY · NOV

APR · AUG · DEC

JAN · MAY · SEPT

FEB · JUNE · OCT

MAR · JULY · NOV

APR · AUG · DEC

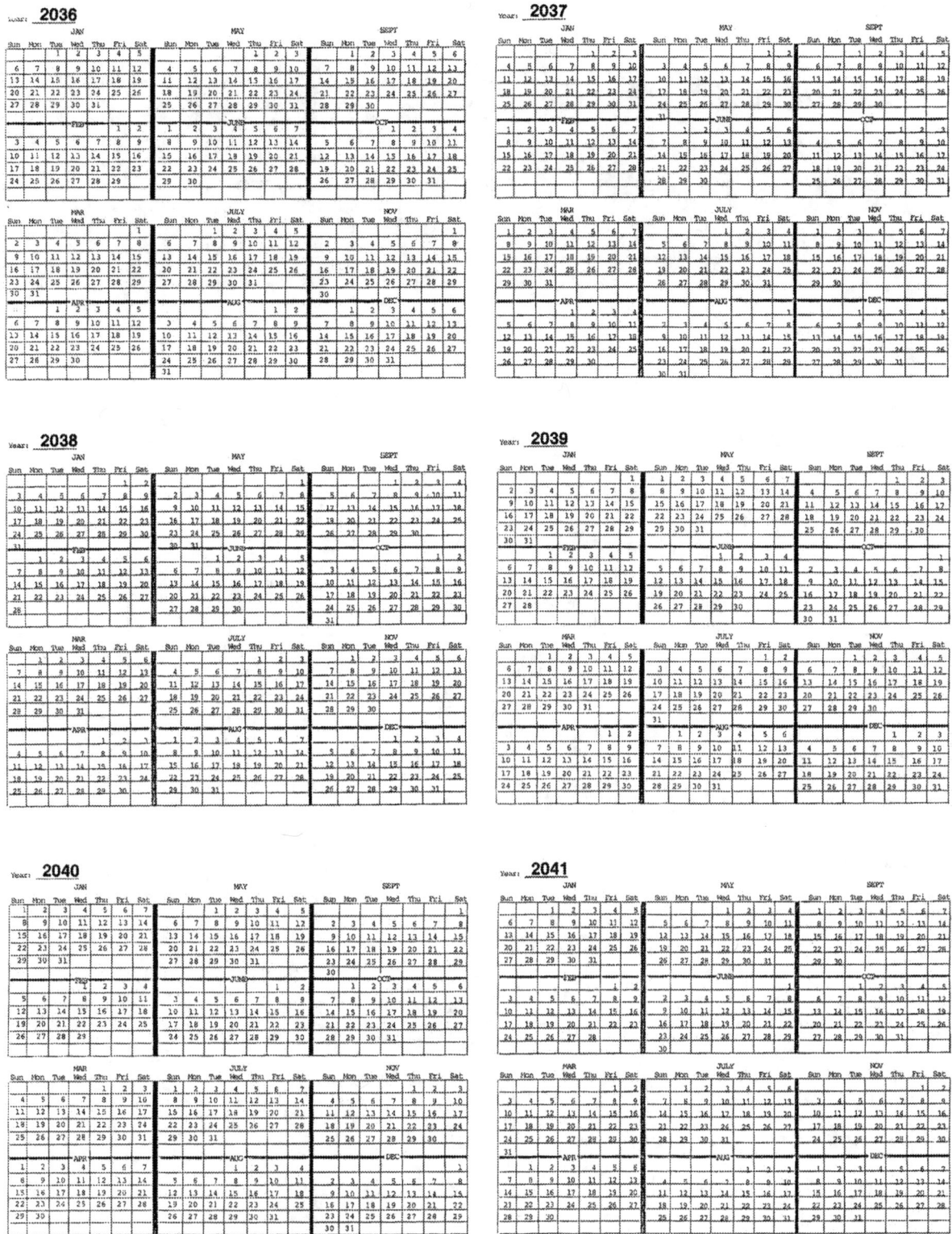

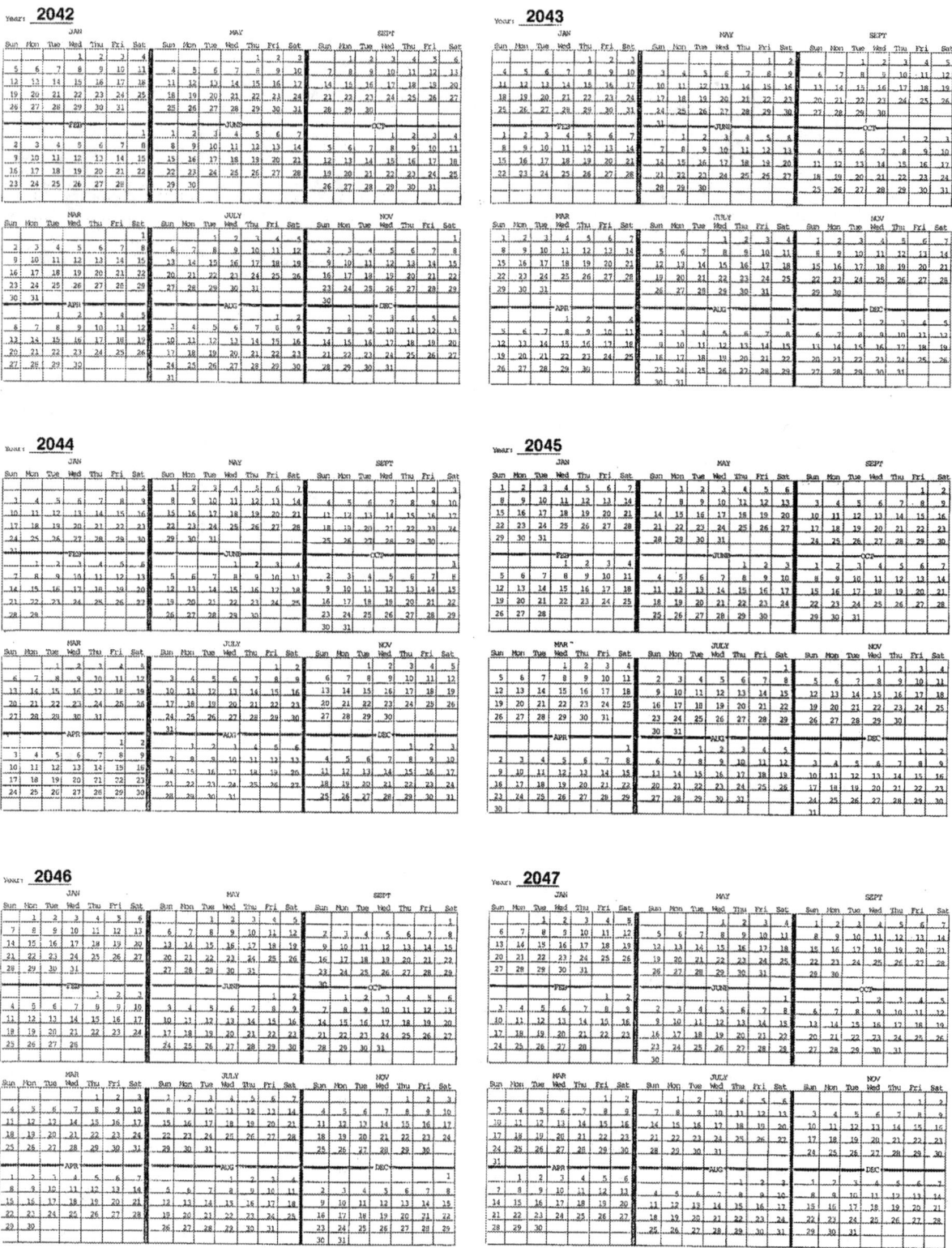

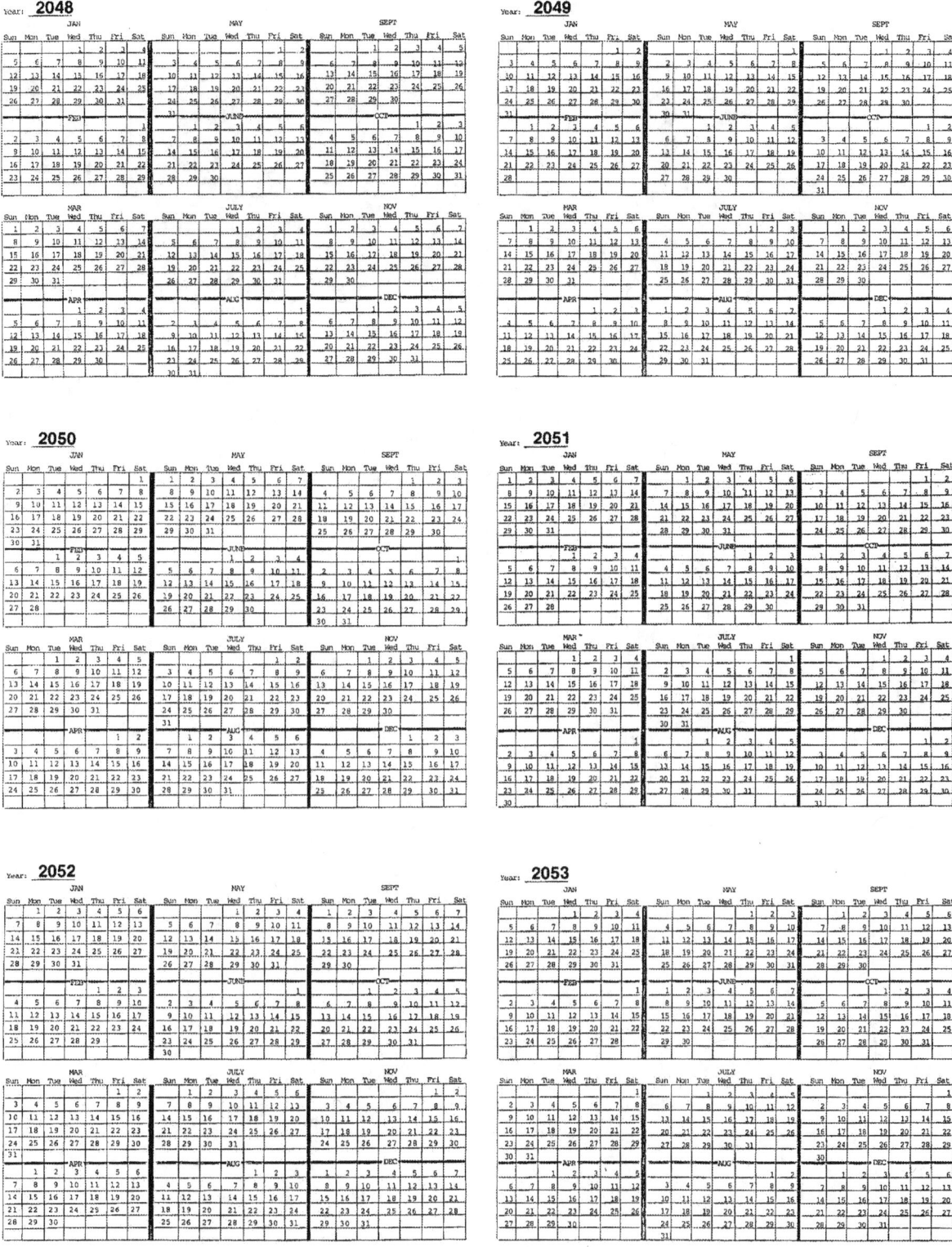

51

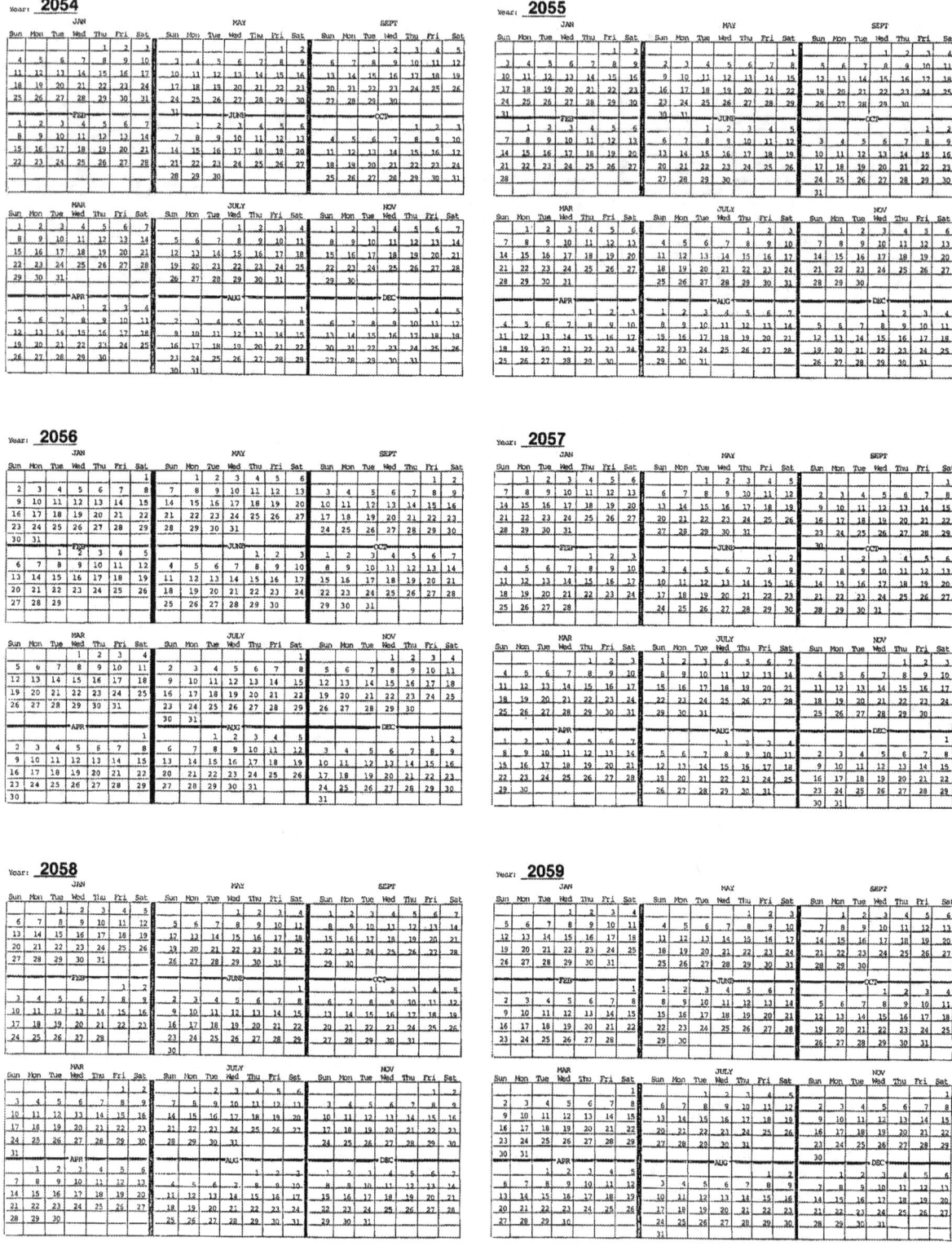

Year: **2054**

Year: **2055**

Year: **2056**

Year: **2057**

Year: **2058**

Year: **2059**

52

Year: **2060**

JAN

Sun	Mon	Tue	Wed	Thu	Fri	Sat
				1	2	3
4	5	6	7	8	9	10
11	12	13	14	15	16	17
18	19	20	21	22	23	24
25	26	27	28	29	30	31

FEB

Sun	Mon	Tue	Wed	Thu	Fri	Sat
1	2	3	4	5	6	7
8	9	10	11	12	13	14
15	16	17	18	19	20	21
22	23	24	25	26	27	28
29						

MAR

Sun	Mon	Tue	Wed	Thu	Fri	Sat
	1	2	3	4	5	6
7	8	9	10	11	12	13
14	15	16	17	18	19	20
21	22	23	24	25	26	27
28	29	30	31			

APR

Sun	Mon	Tue	Wed	Thu	Fri	Sat
				1	2	3
4	5	6	7	8	9	10
11	12	13	14	15	16	17
18	19	20	21	22	23	24
25	26	27	28	29	30	

MAY

Sun	Mon	Tue	Wed	Thu	Fri	Sat
						1
2	3	4	5	6	7	8
9	10	11	12	13	14	15
16	17	18	19	20	21	22
23	24	25	26	27	28	29
30	31					

JUNE

Sun	Mon	Tue	Wed	Thu	Fri	Sat
		1	2	3	4	5
6	7	8	9	10	11	12
13	14	15	16	17	18	19
20	21	22	23	24	25	26
27	28	29	30			

JULY

Sun	Mon	Tue	Wed	Thu	Fri	Sat
				1	2	3
4	5	6	7	8	9	10
11	12	13	14	15	16	17
18	19	20	21	22	23	24
25	26	27	28	29	30	31

AUG

Sun	Mon	Tue	Wed	Thu	Fri	Sat
1	2	3	4	5	6	7
8	9	10	11	12	13	14
15	16	17	18	19	20	21
22	23	24	25	26	27	28
29	30	31				

SEPT

Sun	Mon	Tue	Wed	Thu	Fri	Sat
			1	2	3	4
5	6	7	8	9	10	11
12	13	14	15	16	17	18
19	20	21	22	23	24	25
26	27	28	29	30		

OCT

Sun	Mon	Tue	Wed	Thu	Fri	Sat
					1	2
3	4	5	6	7	8	9
10	11	12	13	14	15	16
17	18	19	20	21	22	23
24	25	26	27	28	29	30
31						

NOV

Sun	Mon	Tue	Wed	Thu	Fri	Sat
	1	2	3	4	5	6
7	8	9	10	11	12	13
14	15	16	17	18	19	20
21	22	23	24	25	26	27
28	29	30				

DEC

Sun	Mon	Tue	Wed	Thu	Fri	Sat
			1	2	3	4
5	6	7	8	9	10	11
12	13	14	15	16	17	18
19	20	21	22	23	24	25
26	27	28	29	30	31	

The Koay Calendar Formula

By application of this formula you will be able to find any day of the week in seconds without looking at a calendar.

The Koay Formula is

$$\frac{M^D + M^C}{7} = W^D$$

M^D = Day of the month

M^C = Constant Number of the month (see table)

W^D = The day of the week (also known as the "remainder" after the division of the Formula shown above).

W^D (the remainder) = 1 is Monday

= 2 is Tuesday

= 3 is Wednesday

= 4 is Thursday

= 5 is Friday

= 6 is Saturday

= 0 is Sunday

If the sum of M^D and M^C is smaller than 7 (seven) then the sum of M^D and M^C is equal to W^D.

$$M^D + M^C = W^D$$

Then division of M^D and M^C by 7 (seven) is not necessary.

54

The Koay Calendar Formula

If the sum of M^D and M^C is 7 or greater than 7 then it is necessary to divide it by 7. The remainder or W^D then is zero and it is Sunday.

Example I:

President John F. Kennedy was born on May 29, 1917.

$M^D = 29$ (day of May)

$M^C = 01$ (i.e. Constant Number of May 1917 from the table)

Therefore, W^D (Remainder) $= 7 \ / \ \overline{29 + 1}$

$$
\begin{array}{r}
4 \\
= 7 \ / \ 30 \\
\underline{28} \\
2 \ \ldots\ldots\text{remainder} = W^D
\end{array}
$$

Here $W^D = 2$

Therefore, May 29, 1917 is on Tuesday.

Example II:

New Year's Day of 2010 (i.e. January 01, 2010)

$M^D = 1$ (day of January)

$M^C = 4$ (i.e. Constant Number of January 2010 from the table)

$W^D = 1 + 4 = 5$

Since the sum of $M^D + M^C$ is smaller than 7, division of the sum is not necessary.

Here $W^D = 5$

Therefore, January 01, 2010 is on Friday.

The Koay Calendar Formula

Example III:

Christmas Day of 2020 (i.e., December 25, 2020)

$M^D = 25$ (day of December)

$M^C = 1$ (i.e. Constant Number of December 2020 from the table)

$$W^D = 7\overline{\smash{)}25+1} = 7\overline{\smash{)}26} \begin{array}{l} 3 \\ \\ \underline{21} \\ 5 \ \text{.......remainder} = W^D \end{array}$$

Here $W^D = 5$

Therefore, December 25, 2020 is on Friday.

Constant Numbers

Year	Jan	Feb	Mar	April	May	June	July	Aug.	Sept.	Oct	Nov.	Dec.
1760	1	4	5	1	3	6	1	4	0	2	5	0
1761	3	6	6	2	4	0	2	5	1	3	6	1
1762	4	0	0	3	5	1	3	6	2	4	0	2
1763	5	1	1	4	6	2	4	0	3	5	1	3
1764	6	2	3	6	1	4	6	2	5	0	3	5
1765	1	4	4	0	2	5	0	3	6	1	4	6

Year	Jan	Feb	Mar	April	May	June	July	Aug.	Sept.	Oct	Nov.	Dec.
1766	2	5	5	1	3	6	1	4	0	2	5	0
1767	3	6	6	2	4	0	2	5	1	3	6	1
1768	4	0	1	4	6	2	4	0	3	5	1	3
1769	6	2	2	5	0	3	5	1	4	6	2	4
1770	0	3	3	6	1	4	6	2	5	0	3	5
1771	1	4	4	0	2	5	0	3	6	1	4	6

Year	Jan	Feb	Mar	April	May	June	July	Aug.	Sept.	Oct	Nov.	Dec.
1772	2	5	6	2	4	0	2	5	1	3	6	1
1773	4	0	0	3	5	1	3	6	2	4	0	2
1774	5	1	1	4	6	2	4	0	3	5	1	3
1775	6	2	2	5	0	3	5	1	4	6	2	4
1776	0	3	4	0	2	5	0	3	6	1	4	6
1777	2	5	5	1	3	6	1	4	0	2	5	0

Year	Jan	Feb	Mar	April	May	June	July	Aug.	Sept.	Oct	Nov.	Dec.
1778	3	6	6	2	4	0	2	5	1	3	6	1
1779	4	0	0	3	5	1	3	6	2	4	0	2
1780	5	1	2	5	0	3	5	1	4	6	2	4
1781	0	3	3	6	1	4	6	2	5	0	3	5
1782	1	4	4	0	2	5	0	3	6	1	4	6
1783	2	5	5	1	3	6	1	4	0	2	5	0

Year	Jan	Feb	Mar	April	May	June	July	Aug.	Sept.	Oct	Nov.	Dec.
1784	3	6	0	3	5	1	3	6	2	4	0	2
1785	5	1	1	4	6	2	4	0	3	5	1	3
1786	6	2	2	5	0	3	5	1	4	6	2	4
1787	0	3	3	6	1	4	6	2	5	0	3	5
1788	1	4	5	1	3	6	1	4	0	2	5	0
1789	3	6	6	2	4	0	2	5	1	3	6	1

Constant Numbers

Year	Jan	Feb	Mar	April	May	June	July	Aug.	Sept.	Oct	Nov.	Dec.
1790	4	0	0	3	5	1	3	6	2	4	0	2
1791	5	1	1	4	6	2	4	0	3	5	1	3
1792	6	2	3	6	1	4	6	2	5	0	3	5
1793	1	4	4	0	2	5	0	3	6	1	4	6
1794	2	5	5	1	3	6	1	4	0	2	5	0
1795	3	6	6	2	4	0	2	5	1	3	6	1

Year	Jan	Feb	Mar	April	May	June	July	Aug.	Sept.	Oct	Nov.	Dec.
1796	4	0	1	4	6	2	4	0	3	5	1	3
1797	6	2	2	5	0	3	5	1	4	6	2	4
1798	0	3	3	6	1	4	6	2	5	0	3	5
1799	1	4	4	0	2	5	0	3	6	1	4	6
1800	2	5	5	1	3	6	1	4	0	2	5	0
1801	3	6	6	2	4	0	2	5	1	3	6	1

Year	Jan	Feb	Mar	April	May	June	July	Aug.	Sept.	Oct	Nov.	Dec.
1802	4	0	0	3	5	1	3	6	2	4	0	2
1803	5	1	1	4	6	2	4	0	3	5	1	3
1804	6	2	3	6	1	4	6	2	5	0	3	5
1805	1	4	4	0	2	5	0	3	6	1	4	6
1806	2	5	5	1	3	6	1	4	0	2	5	0
1807	3	6	6	2	4	0	2	5	1	3	6	1

Year	Jan	Feb	Mar	April	May	June	July	Aug.	Sept.	Oct	Nov.	Dec.
1808	4	0	1	4	6	2	4	0	3	5	1	3
1809	6	2	2	5	0	3	5	1	4	6	2	4
1810	0	3	3	6	1	4	6	2	5	0	3	5
1811	1	4	4	0	2	5	0	3	6	1	4	6
1812	2	5	6	2	4	0	2	5	1	3	6	1
1813	4	0	0	3	5	1	3	6	2	4	0	2

Year	Jan	Feb	Mar	April	May	June	July	Aug.	Sept.	Oct	Nov.	Dec.
1814	5	1	1	4	6	2	4	0	3	5	1	3
1815	6	2	2	5	0	3	5	1	4	6	2	4
1816	0	3	4	0	2	5	0	3	6	1	4	6
1817	2	5	5	1	3	6	1	4	0	2	5	0
1818	3	6	6	2	4	0	2	5	1	3	6	1
1819	4	0	0	3	5	1	3	6	2	4	0	2

Constant Numbers

Year	Jan	Feb	Mar	April	May	June	July	Aug.	Sept.	Oct	Nov.	Dec.
1820	5	1	2	5	0	3	5	1	4	6	2	4
1821	0	3	3	6	1	4	6	2	5	0	3	5
1822	1	4	4	0	2	5	0	3	6	1	4	6
1823	2	5	5	1	3	6	1	4	0	2	5	0
1824	3	6	0	3	5	1	3	6	2	4	0	2
1825	5	1	1	4	6	2	4	0	3	5	1	3

Year	Jan	Feb	Mar	April	May	June	July	Aug.	Sept.	Oct	Nov.	Dec.
1826	6	2	2	5	0	3	5	1	4	6	2	4
1827	0	3	3	6	1	4	6	2	5	0	3	5
1828	1	4	5	1	3	6	1	4	0	2	5	0
1829	3	6	6	2	4	0	2	5	1	3	6	1
1830	4	0	0	3	5	1	3	6	2	4	0	2
1831	5	1	1	4	6	2	4	0	3	5	1	3

Year	Jan	Feb	Mar	April	May	June	July	Aug.	Sept.	Oct	Nov.	Dec.
1832	6	2	3	6	1	4	6	2	5	0	3	5
1833	1	4	4	0	2	5	0	3	6	1	4	6
1834	2	5	5	1	3	6	1	4	0	2	5	0
1835	3	6	6	2	4	0	2	5	1	3	6	1
1836	4	0	1	4	6	2	4	0	3	5	1	3
1837	6	2	2	5	0	3	5	1	4	6	2	4

Year	Jan	Feb	Mar	April	May	June	July	Aug.	Sept.	Oct	Nov.	Dec.
1838	0	3	3	6	1	4	6	2	5	0	3	5
1839	1	4	4	0	2	5	0	3	6	1	4	6
1840	2	5	6	2	4	0	2	5	1	3	6	1
1841	4	0	0	3	5	1	3	6	2	4	0	2
1842	5	1	1	4	6	2	4	0	3	5	1	3
1843	6	2	2	5	0	3	5	1	4	6	2	4

Year	Jan	Feb	Mar	April	May	June	July	Aug.	Sept.	Oct	Nov.	Dec.
1844	0	3	4	0	2	5	0	3	6	1	4	6
1845	2	5	5	1	3	6	1	4	0	2	5	0
1846	3	6	6	2	4	0	2	5	1	3	6	1
1847	4	0	0	3	5	1	3	6	2	4	0	2
1848	5	1	2	5	0	3	5	1	4	6	2	4
1849	0	3	3	6	1	4	6	2	5	0	3	5

Constant Numbers

Year	Jan	Feb	Mar	April	May	June	July	Aug.	Sept.	Oct	Nov.	Dec.
1850	1	4	4	0	2	5	0	3	6	1	4	6
1851	2	5	5	1	3	6	1	4	0	2	5	0
1852	3	6	0	3	5	1	3	6	2	4	0	2
1853	5	1	1	4	6	2	4	0	3	5	1	3
1854	6	2	2	5	0	3	5	1	4	6	2	4
1855	0	3	3	6	1	4	6	2	5	0	3	5

Year	Jan	Feb	Mar	April	May	June	July	Aug.	Sept.	Oct	Nov.	Dec.
1856	1	4	5	1	3	6	1	4	0	2	5	0
1857	3	6	6	2	4	0	2	5	1	3	6	1
1858	4	0	0	3	5	1	3	6	2	4	0	2
1859	5	1	1	4	6	2	4	0	3	5	1	3
1860	6	2	3	6	1	4	6	2	5	0	3	5
1861	1	4	4	0	2	5	0	3	6	1	4	6

Year	Jan	Feb	Mar	April	May	June	July	Aug.	Sept.	Oct	Nov.	Dec.
1862	2	5	5	1	3	6	1	4	0	2	5	0
1863	3	6	6	2	4	0	2	5	1	3	6	1
1864	4	0	1	4	6	2	4	0	3	5	1	3
1865	6	2	2	5	0	3	5	1	4	6	2	4
1866	0	3	3	6	1	4	6	2	5	0	3	5
1867	1	4	4	0	2	5	0	3	6	1	4	6

Year	Jan	Feb	Mar	April	May	June	July	Aug.	Sept.	Oct	Nov.	Dec.
1868	2	5	6	2	4	0	2	5	1	3	6	1
1869	4	0	0	3	5	1	3	6	2	4	0	2
1870	5	1	1	4	6	2	4	0	3	5	1	3
1871	6	2	2	5	0	3	5	1	4	6	2	4
1872	0	3	4	0	2	5	0	3	6	1	4	6
1873	2	5	5	1	3	6	1	4	0	2	5	0

Year	Jan	Feb	Mar	April	May	June	July	Aug.	Sept.	Oct	Nov.	Dec.
1874	3	6	6	2	4	0	2	5	1	3	6	1
1875	4	0	0	3	5	1	3	6	2	4	0	2
1876	5	1	2	5	0	3	5	1	4	6	2	4
1877	0	3	3	6	1	4	6	2	5	0	3	5
1878	1	4	4	0	2	5	0	3	6	1	4	6
1879	2	5	5	1	3	6	1	4	0	2	5	0

Constant Numbers

Year	Jan	Feb	Mar	April	May	June	July	Aug.	Sept.	Oct	Nov.	Dec.
1880	3	6	0	3	5	1	3	6	2	4	0	2
1881	5	1	1	4	6	2	4	0	3	5	1	3
1882	6	2	2	5	0	3	5	1	4	6	2	4
1883	0	3	3	6	1	4	6	2	5	0	3	5
1884	1	4	5	1	3	6	1	4	0	2	5	0
1885	3	6	6	2	4	0	2	5	1	3	6	1

Year	Jan	Feb	Mar	April	May	June	July	Aug.	Sept.	Oct	Nov.	Dec.
1886	4	0	0	3	5	1	3	6	2	4	0	2
1887	5	1	1	4	6	2	4	0	3	5	1	3
1888	6	2	3	6	1	4	6	2	5	0	3	5
1889	1	4	4	0	2	5	0	3	6	1	4	6
1890	2	5	5	1	3	6	1	4	0	2	5	0
1891	3	6	6	2	4	0	2	5	1	3	6	1

Year	Jan	Feb	Mar	April	May	June	July	Aug.	Sept.	Oct	Nov.	Dec.
1892	4	0	1	4	6	2	4	0	3	5	1	3
1893	6	2	2	5	0	3	5	1	4	6	2	4
1894	0	3	3	6	1	4	6	2	5	0	3	5
1895	1	4	4	0	2	5	0	3	6	1	4	6
1896	2	5	6	2	4	0	2	5	1	3	6	1
1897	4	0	0	3	5	1	3	6	2	4	0	2

Year	Jan	Feb	Mar	April	May	June	July	Aug.	Sept.	Oct	Nov.	Dec.
1898	5	1	1	4	6	2	4	0	3	5	1	3
1899	6	2	2	5	0	3	5	1	4	6	2	4
1900	0	3	3	6	1	4	6	2	5	0	3	5
1901	1	4	4	0	2	5	0	3	6	1	4	6
1902	2	5	5	1	3	6	1	4	0	2	5	0
1903	3	6	6	2	4	0	2	5	1	3	6	1

Year	Jan	Feb	Mar	April	May	June	July	Aug.	Sept.	Oct	Nov.	Dec.
1904	4	0	1	4	6	2	4	0	3	5	1	3
1905	6	2	2	5	0	3	5	1	4	6	2	4
1906	0	3	3	6	1	4	6	2	5	0	3	5
1907	1	4	4	0	2	5	0	3	6	1	4	6
1908	2	5	6	2	4	0	2	5	1	3	6	1
1909	4	0	0	3	5	1	3	6	2	4	0	2

Constant Numbers

Year	Jan	Feb	Mar	April	May	June	July	Aug.	Sept.	Oct	Nov.	Dec.
1910	5	1	1	4	6	2	4	0	3	5	1	3
1911	6	2	2	5	0	3	5	1	4	6	2	4
1912	0	3	4	0	2	5	0	3	6	1	4	6
1913	2	5	5	1	3	6	1	4	0	2	5	0
1914	3	6	6	2	4	0	2	5	1	3	6	1
1915	4	0	0	3	5	1	3	6	2	4	0	2

Year	Jan	Feb	Mar	April	May	June	July	Aug.	Sept.	Oct	Nov.	Dec.
1916	5	1	2	5	0	3	5	1	4	6	2	4
1917	0	3	3	6	1	4	6	2	5	0	3	5
1918	1	4	4	0	2	5	0	3	6	1	4	6
1919	2	5	5	1	3	6	1	4	0	2	5	0
1920	3	6	0	3	5	1	3	6	2	4	0	2
1921	5	1	1	4	6	2	4	0	3	5	1	3

Year	Jan	Feb	Mar	April	May	June	July	Aug.	Sept.	Oct	Nov.	Dec.
1922	6	2	2	5	0	3	5	1	4	6	2	4
1923	0	3	3	6	1	4	6	2	5	0	3	5
1924	1	4	5	1	3	6	1	4	0	2	5	0
1925	3	6	6	2	4	0	2	5	1	3	6	1
1926	4	0	0	3	5	1	3	6	2	4	0	2
1927	5	1	1	4	6	2	4	0	3	5	1	3

Year	Jan	Feb	Mar	April	May	June	July	Aug.	Sept.	Oct	Nov.	Dec.
1928	6	2	3	6	1	4	6	2	5	0	3	5
1929	1	4	4	0	2	5	0	3	6	1	4	6
1930	2	5	5	1	3	6	1	4	0	2	5	0
1931	3	6	6	2	4	0	2	5	1	3	6	1
1932	4	0	1	4	6	2	4	0	3	5	1	3
1933	6	2	2	5	0	3	5	1	4	6	2	4

Year	Jan	Feb	Mar	April	May	June	July	Aug.	Sept.	Oct	Nov.	Dec.
1934	0	3	3	6	1	4	6	2	5	0	3	5
1935	1	4	4	0	2	5	0	3	6	1	4	6
1936	2	5	6	2	4	0	2	5	1	3	6	1
1937	4	0	0	3	5	1	3	6	2	4	0	2
1938	5	1	1	4	6	2	4	0	3	5	1	3
1939	6	2	2	5	0	3	5	1	4	6	2	4

Constant Numbers

Year	Jan	Feb	Mar	April	May	June	July	Aug.	Sept.	Oct	Nov.	Dec.
1940	0	3	4	0	2	5	0	3	6	1	4	6
1941	2	5	5	1	3	6	1	4	0	2	5	0
1942	3	6	6	2	4	0	2	5	1	3	6	1
1943	4	0	0	3	5	1	3	6	2	4	0	2
1944	5	1	2	5	0	3	5	1	4	6	2	4
1945	0	3	3	6	1	4	6	2	5	0	3	5

Year	Jan	Feb	Mar	April	May	June	July	Aug.	Sept.	Oct	Nov.	Dec.
1946	1	4	4	0	2	5	0	3	6	1	4	6
1947	2	5	5	1	3	6	1	4	0	2	5	0
1948	3	6	0	3	5	1	3	6	2	4	0	2
1949	5	1	1	4	6	2	4	0	3	5	1	3
1950	6	2	2	5	0	3	5	1	4	6	2	4
1951	0	3	3	6	1	4	6	2	5	0	3	5

Year	Jan	Feb	Mar	April	May	June	July	Aug.	Sept.	Oct	Nov.	Dec.
1952	1	4	5	1	3	6	1	4	0	2	5	0
1953	3	6	6	2	4	0	2	5	1	3	6	1
1954	4	0	0	3	5	1	3	6	2	4	0	2
1955	5	1	1	4	6	2	4	0	3	5	1	3
1956	6	2	3	6	1	4	6	2	5	0	3	5
1957	1	4	4	0	2	5	0	3	6	1	4	6

Year	Jan	Feb	Mar	April	May	June	July	Aug.	Sept.	Oct	Nov.	Dec.
1958	2	5	5	1	3	6	1	4	0	2	5	0
1959	3	6	6	2	4	0	2	5	1	3	6	1
1960	4	0	1	4	6	2	4	0	3	5	1	3
1961	6	2	2	5	0	3	5	1	4	6	2	4
1962	0	3	3	6	1	4	6	2	5	0	3	5
1963	1	4	4	0	2	5	0	3	6	1	4	6

Year	Jan	Feb	Mar	April	May	June	July	Aug.	Sept.	Oct	Nov.	Dec.
1964	2	5	6	2	4	0	2	5	1	3	6	1
1965	4	0	0	3	5	1	3	6	2	4	0	2
1966	5	1	1	4	6	2	4	0	3	5	1	3
1967	6	2	2	5	0	3	5	1	4	6	2	4
1968	0	3	4	0	2	5	0	3	6	1	4	6
1969	2	5	5	1	3	6	1	4	0	2	5	0

Constant Numbers

Year	Jan	Feb	Mar	April	May	June	July	Aug.	Sept.	Oct	Nov.	Dec.
1970	3	6	6	2	4	0	2	5	1	3	6	1
1971	4	0	0	3	5	1	3	6	2	4	0	2
1972	5	1	2	5	0	3	5	1	4	6	2	4
1973	0	3	3	6	1	4	6	2	5	0	3	5
1974	1	4	4	0	2	5	0	3	6	1	4	6
1975	2	5	5	1	3	6	1	4	0	2	5	0

Year	Jan	Feb	Mar	April	May	June	July	Aug.	Sept.	Oct	Nov.	Dec.
1976	3	6	0	3	5	1	3	6	2	4	0	2
1977	5	1	1	4	6	2	4	0	3	5	1	3
1978	6	2	2	5	0	3	5	1	4	6	2	4
1979	0	3	3	6	1	4	6	2	5	0	3	5
1980	1	4	5	1	3	6	1	4	0	2	5	0
1981	3	6	6	2	4	0	2	5	1	3	6	1

Year	Jan	Feb	Mar	April	May	June	July	Aug.	Sept.	Oct	Nov.	Dec.
1982	4	0	0	3	5	1	3	6	2	4	0	2
1983	5	1	1	4	6	2	4	0	3	5	1	3
1984	6	2	3	6	1	4	6	2	5	0	3	5
1985	1	4	4	0	2	5	0	3	6	1	4	6
1986	2	5	5	1	3	6	1	4	0	2	5	0
1987	3	6	6	2	4	0	2	5	1	3	6	1

Year	Jan	Feb	Mar	April	May	June	July	Aug.	Sept.	Oct	Nov.	Dec.
1988	4	0	1	4	6	2	4	0	3	5	1	3
1989	6	2	2	5	0	3	5	1	4	6	2	4
1990	0	3	3	6	1	4	6	2	5	0	3	5
1991	1	4	4	0	2	5	0	3	6	1	4	6
1992	2	5	6	2	4	0	2	5	1	3	6	1
1993	4	0	0	3	5	1	3	6	2	4	0	2

Year	Jan	Feb	Mar	April	May	June	July	Aug.	Sept.	Oct	Nov.	Dec.
1994	5	1	1	4	6	2	4	0	3	5	1	3
1995	6	2	2	5	0	3	5	1	4	6	2	4
1996	0	3	4	0	2	5	0	3	6	1	4	6
1997	2	5	5	1	3	6	1	4	0	2	5	0
1998	3	6	6	2	4	0	2	5	1	3	6	1
1999	4	0	0	3	5	1	3	6	2	4	0	2

Constant Numbers

Year	Jan	Feb	Mar	April	May	June	July	Aug.	Sept.	Oct	Nov.	Dec.
2000	5	1	2	5	0	3	5	1	4	6	2	4
2001	0	3	3	6	1	4	6	2	5	0	3	5
2002	1	4	4	0	2	5	0	3	6	1	4	6
2003	2	5	5	1	3	6	1	4	0	2	5	0
2004	3	6	0	3	5	1	3	6	2	4	0	2
2005	5	1	1	4	6	2	4	0	3	5	1	3

Year	Jan	Feb	Mar	April	May	June	July	Aug.	Sept.	Oct	Nov.	Dec.
2006	6	2	2	5	0	3	5	1	4	6	2	4
2007	0	3	3	6	1	4	6	2	5	0	3	5
2008	1	4	5	1	3	6	1	4	0	2	5	0
2009	3	6	6	2	4	0	2	5	1	3	6	1
2010	4	0	0	3	5	1	3	6	2	4	0	2
2011	5	1	1	4	6	2	4	0	3	5	1	3

Year	Jan	Feb	Mar	April	May	June	July	Aug.	Sept.	Oct	Nov.	Dec.
2012	6	2	3	6	1	4	6	2	5	0	3	5
2013	1	4	4	0	2	5	0	3	6	1	4	6
2014	2	5	5	1	3	6	1	4	0	2	5	0
2015	3	6	6	2	4	0	2	5	1	3	6	1
2016	4	0	1	4	6	2	4	0	3	5	1	3
2017	6	2	2	5	0	3	5	1	4	6	2	4

Year	Jan	Feb	Mar	April	May	June	July	Aug.	Sept.	Oct	Nov.	Dec.
2018	0	3	3	6	1	4	6	2	5	0	3	5
2019	1	4	4	0	2	5	0	3	6	1	4	6
2020	2	5	6	2	4	0	2	5	1	3	6	1
2021	4	0	0	3	5	1	3	6	2	4	0	2
2022	5	1	1	4	6	2	4	0	3	5	1	3
2023	6	2	2	5	0	3	5	1	4	6	2	4

Year	Jan	Feb	Mar	April	May	June	July	Aug.	Sept.	Oct	Nov.	Dec.
2024	0	3	4	0	2	5	0	3	6	1	4	6
2025	2	5	5	1	3	6	1	4	0	2	5	0
2026	3	6	6	2	4	0	2	5	1	3	6	1
2027	4	0	0	3	5	1	3	6	2	4	0	2
2028	5	1	2	5	0	3	5	1	4	6	2	4
2029	0	3	3	6	1	4	6	2	5	0	3	5

Constant Numbers

Year	Jan	Feb	Mar	April	May	June	July	Aug.	Sept.	Oct	Nov.	Dec.
2030	1	4	4	0	2	5	0	3	6	1	4	6
2031	2	5	5	1	3	6	1	4	0	2	5	0
2032	3	6	0	3	5	1	3	6	2	4	0	2
2033	5	1	1	4	6	2	4	0	3	5	1	3
2034	6	2	2	5	0	3	5	1	4	6	2	4
2035	0	3	3	6	1	4	6	2	5	0	3	5

Year	Jan	Feb	Mar	April	May	June	July	Aug.	Sept.	Oct	Nov.	Dec.
2036	1	4	5	1	3	6	1	4	0	2	5	0
2037	3	6	6	2	4	0	2	5	1	3	6	1
2038	4	0	0	3	5	1	3	6	2	4	0	2
2039	5	1	1	4	6	2	4	0	3	5	1	3
2040	6	2	3	6	1	4	6	2	5	0	3	5
2041	1	4	4	0	2	5	0	3	6	1	4	6

Year	Jan	Feb	Mar	April	May	June	July	Aug.	Sept.	Oct	Nov.	Dec.
2042	2	5	5	1	3	6	1	4	0	2	5	0
2043	3	6	6	2	4	0	2	5	1	3	6	1
2044	4	0	1	4	6	2	4	0	3	5	1	3
2045	6	2	2	5	0	3	5	1	4	6	2	4
2046	0	3	3	6	1	4	6	2	5	0	3	5
2047	1	4	4	0	2	5	0	3	6	1	4	6

Year	Jan	Feb	Mar	April	May	June	July	Aug.	Sept.	Oct	Nov.	Dec.
2048	2	5	6	2	4	0	2	5	1	3	6	1
2049	4	0	0	3	5	1	3	6	2	4	0	2
2050	5	1	1	4	6	2	4	0	3	5	1	3
2051	6	2	2	5	0	3	5	1	4	6	2	4
2052	0	3	4	0	2	5	0	3	6	1	4	6
2053	2	5	5	1	3	6	1	4	0	2	5	0

Year	Jan	Feb	Mar	April	May	June	July	Aug.	Sept.	Oct	Nov.	Dec.
2054	3	6	6	2	4	0	2	5	1	3	6	1
2055	4	0	0	3	5	1	3	6	2	4	0	2
2056	5	1	2	5	0	3	5	1	4	6	2	4
2057	0	3	3	6	1	4	6	2	5	0	3	5
2058	1	4	4	0	2	5	0	3	6	1	4	6
2059	2	5	5	1	3	6	1	4	0	2	5	0
2060	3	6	0	3	5	1	3	6	2	4	0	2

The Presidents of the United States

President	Born		President	Born	
1. Washington, George	Feb. 22, 1732	Fri	23. Harrison, Benjamin	Aug. 20, 1833	Tue
2. Adams, John	Oct. 30, 1735	Sun	24. Cleveland, Grover	Mar. 18, 1837	Sat
3. Jefferson, Thomas	Apr. 13, 1743	Sat	25. McKinley, William	Jan. 29, 1843	Sun
4. Madison, James	Mar. 16, 1751	Tue	26. Roosevelt, Theodore	Oct. 27, 1858	Wed
5. Monroe, James	Apr. 28, 1758	Fri	27. Taft, William H.	Sept. 15, 1857	Tue
6. Adams, John Quincy	July 11, 1767	Sat	28. Wilson, Woodrow	Dec. 28, 1856	Sun
7. Jackson, Andrew	Mar. 15, 1767	Sun	29. Harding, Warren G.	Nov. 2, 1865	Thu
8. Buren, Martin Van	Dec. 05, 1782	Thu	30. Coolidge, Calvin	July 4, 1872	Thu
9. Harrison, William H.	Feb. 09, 1773	Tue	31. Hoover, Herbert C.	Aug. 10, 1874	Mon
10. Tyler, John	Mar. 29, 1790	Mon	32. Roosevelt, Franklin D.	Jan. 30, 1882	Mon
11. Polk, James K.	Nov. 02, 1795	Mon	33. Truman, Harry S.	May 8, 1884	Thu
12. Taylor, Zachary	Nov. 24, 1784	Wed	34. Eisenhower, Dwight D.	Oct. 14, 1890	Tue
13. Fillmore, Millard	Jan. 07, 1800	Tue	35. Kennedy, John F.	May 29, 1917	Tue
14. Pierce, Franklin	Nov. 23, 1804	Fri	36. Johnson, Lyndon B.	Aug. 27, 1908	Thu
15. Buchanan, James	April 23, 1791	Sat	37. Nixon, Richard M.	Jan. 9, 1913	Thu
16. Lincoln, Abraham	Feb. 12, 1809	Sun	38. Ford, Gerald R.	July 14, 1913	Mon
17. Johnson, Andrew	Dec. 29, 1808	Thu	39. Carter Jr., James E.	Oct. 1, 1924	Wed
18. Grant, Ulysses S.	Apr. 27, 1822	Sat	40. Reagan, Ronald W.	Feb. 6, 1911	Mon
19. Hayes, Rutherford B.	Oct. 04, 1822	Fri	41. Bush, George Herbert Walker	June 12, 1924	Thu
20. Garfield, James A.	Nov. 19, 1831	Sat	42. Clinton, Bill J.	Aug. 19, 1946	Mon
21. Arthur, Chester A.	Oct. 05, 1830	Tue	43. Bush, George W.	July 6, 1946	Sat
22. Cleveland, Grover	Mar. 18, 1837	Sat			

www.ingramcontent.com/pod-product-compliance
Lightning Source LLC
Chambersburg PA
CBHW052009280526
45793CB00005B/909